Frommer's®

London
day BY day®

3rd Edition

by Joe Fullman

WILEY

John Wiley & Sons, Inc.

Contents

DISCARD

Copyright © 2012 John Wiley & Sons, Inc, The Atrium, Southern Gate,
Chichester, West Sussex PO19 8SQ, England
Telephone (+44) 1243 779777
Email (for orders and customer service enquiries): cs-books@wiley.co.uk. Visit
our Home Page on www.wiley.com

Editorial Director: Kelly Regan
Production Manager: Daniel Mersey
Commissioning Editor: Fiona Quinn
Development Editor: Claire Baranowski
Content Editor: Erica Peters
Photo Research: Cherie Cincilla, Richard H. Fox, Jill Emeny
Cartography: Andrew Murphy

British Library Cataloguing in Publication Data
A catalogue record for this book is available from the British Library

ISBN 978-1-119-99486-2 (pbk), ISBN 978-1-119-97265-5 (ebk),
ISBN 978-1-119-99876-1 (ebk), ISBN 978-1-119-99877-8 (ebk)

Typeset by Wiley Indianapolis Composition Services

Printed and bound in China by RR Donnelley

5 4 3 2 1

A Note from the Editorial Director

Organizing your time. That's what this guide is all about.

Other guides give you long lists of things to see and do and then expect you to fit the pieces together. The Day by Day guides are different. These guides tell you the best of everything, and then they show you how to see it *in the smartest, most time-efficient way.* Our authors have designed detailed itineraries organized by time, neighborhood, or special interest. And each tour comes with a bulleted map that takes you from stop to stop.

Hoping to see where the Queen lives, or the global treasures of the British Museum? Planning a walk through swanky Chelsea, the "New London" of the East End, or the shopping streets of the West End? Whatever your interest or schedule, the Day by Days give you the smartest routes to follow. Not only do we take you to the top attractions, hotels, and restaurants, but we also help you access those special moments that locals get to experience—those "finds" that turn tourists into travelers.

The Day by Days are also your top choice if you're looking for one complete guide for all your travel needs. The best hotels and restaurants for every budget, the greatest shopping values, the wildest nightlife—it's all here.

Why should you trust our judgment? Because our authors personally visit each place they write about. They're an independent lot who say what they think and would never include places they wouldn't recommend to their best friends. They're also open to suggestions from readers. If you'd like to contact them, please send your comments our way at feedback@frommers.com, and we'll pass them on.

Enjoy your Day by Day guide—the most helpful travel companion you can buy. And have the trip of a lifetime.

Warm regards,

Kelly Regan

Kelly Regan, Editorial Director
Frommer's Travel Guides

About the Author

Joe Fullman has lived in London for 39 years—or, to put it another way, all his life. It is, as far as he's concerned, the best city in the world, and having worked as a travel writer for more than a decade, he's had the opportunity to compare it to some very distinguished rivals. Joe has written on destinations including England, Berlin, Venice, Las Vegas, Costa Rica, and Belize. He is the author of Frommer's *London Free & Dirt Cheap* and a contributor to Frommer's *London 2012*.

Acknowledgments

Thanks also to everyone who took the time to answer my queries, sort things out for me, recommend things to me, point me in the right direction, go eating and drinking with me (although that can't have been too much of a chore), and generally find out the best London has to offer. Special cheers to, in no particulary order, mum and dad, Sam, Jon, David, Anna, Ben, Nick, Jayne, Andy, Gary, Barry, and, of course, Fiona for trusting me with the task and being ever-tolerant of my occasional lack of deadline discipline.

Advisory & Disclaimer

Travel information can change quickly and unexpectedly, and we strongly advise you to confirm important details locally before traveling, including information on visas, health and safety, traffic and transport, accommodations, shopping, and eating out. We also encourage you to stay alert while traveling, and to remain aware of your surroundings. Avoid civil disturbances, and keep a close eye on cameras, purses, wallets, and other valuables.

While we have endeavored to ensure that the information contained within this guide is accurate and up-to-date at the time of publication, we make no representations or warranties with respect to the accuracy or completeness of the contents of this work and specifically disclaim all warranties, including without limitation warranties of fitness for a particular purpose. We accept no responsibility or liability for any inaccuracy or errors or omissions, or for any inconvenience, loss, damage, costs, or expenses of any nature whatsoever incurred or suffered by anyone as a result of any advice, or information contained in this guide.

The inclusion of a company, organization or website in this guide as a service provider and/or potential source of further information does not mean that we endorse them or the information they provide. Be aware that information provided through some websites may be unreliable and can change without notice. Neither the publisher nor author shall be liable for any damages arising herefrom.

Star Ratings, Icons & Abbreviations

Every hotel, restaurant, and attraction listing in this guide has been ranked for quality, value, service, amenities, and special features using a **star-rating system.** Hotels, restaurants, attractions, shopping, and nightlife are rated on a scale of zero stars (recommended) to three stars (exceptional). In addition to the star-rating system, we also use a **kids icon** to point out the best bets for families. Within each tour, we recommend cafes, bars, or restaurants where you can take a break with a £ sign to indicate price. Each of these stops appears in a shaded box marked with a coffee-cup-shaped bullet 🍵 .

The following **abbreviations** are used for credit cards:

AE	American Express	DISC	Discover	V	Visa
DC	Diners Club	MC	MasterCard		

Travel Resources at Frommers.com

Frommer's travel resources don't end with this guide. Frommer's website, **www.frommers.com**, has travel information on more than 4,000 destinations. We update features regularly, giving you access to the most current trip-planning information and the best airfare, lodging, and car-rental bargains. You can also listen to podcasts, connect with other Frommers.com members through our active-reader forums, share your travel photos, read blogs from guidebook editors and fellow travelers, and much more.

How to Contact Us

In researching this book, we discovered many wonderful places—hotels, restaurants, shops, and more. We're sure you'll find others. Please tell us about them, so we can share the information with your fellow travelers in upcoming editions. If you were disappointed with a recommendation, we'd love to know that, too. Please e-mail: frommers@wiley.com or write to:

Frommer's London Day by Day, 3rd Edition
John Wiley & Sons, Inc. • 111 River St. • Hoboken, NJ 07030-5774

16 Favorite **Moments**

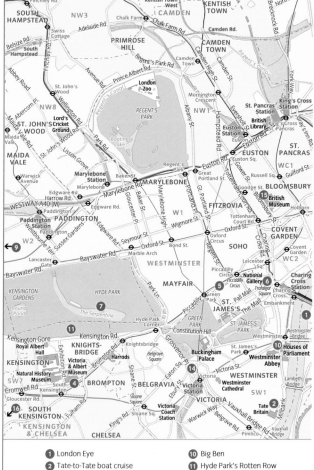

1. London Eye
2. Tate-to-Tate boat cruise
3. Pub crawl through the City
4. The Late View at the V&A
5. The Wolseley
6. National Gallery
7. The Serpentine
8. Vertigo 42
9. Portobello Road Market
10. Big Ben
11. Hyde Park's Rotten Row
12. Millennium Bridge
13. Shakespeare's Globe Theatre
14. The Goring
15. British Museum
16. Hampton Court Palace's Hedge Maze

Previous page: Oxford Street.

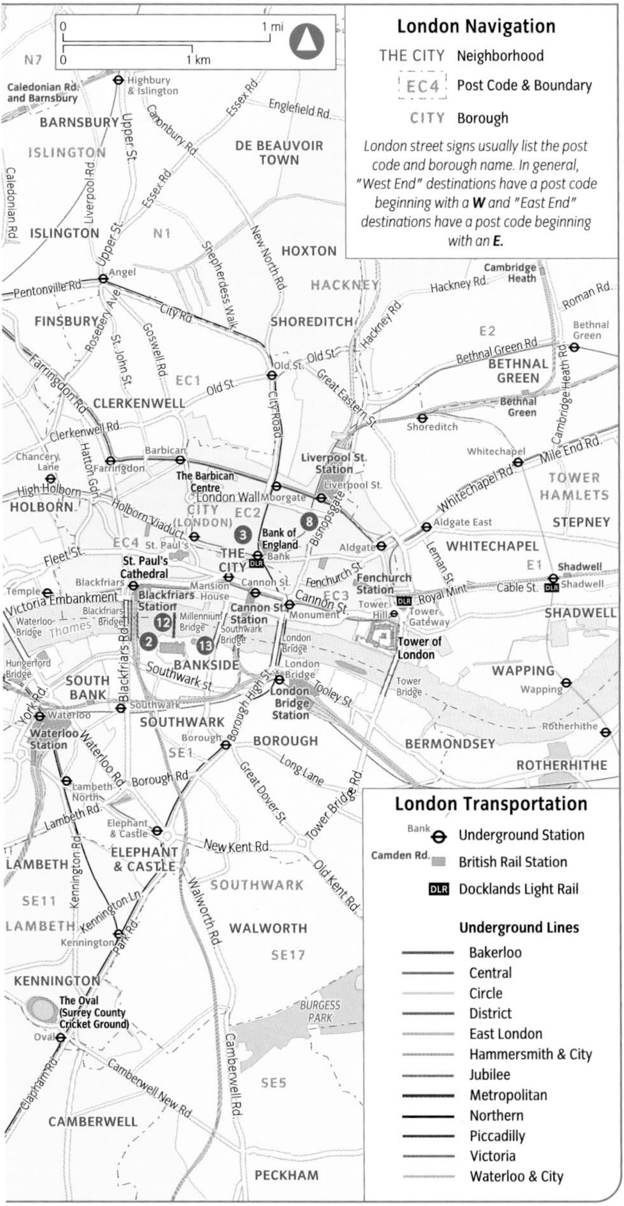
London Navigation
THE CITY Neighborhood
EC4 Post Code & Boundary
CITY Borough
London street signs usually list the post code and borough name. In general, "West End" destinations have a post code beginning with a W and "East End" destinations have a post code beginning with an E.
0 1 mi
0 1 km
N7
Caledonian Rd. and Barnsbury
Highbury & Islington
Essex Rd.
Englefield Rd.
BARNSBURY
Canonbury Rd.
ISLINGTON
Upper St.
DE BEAUVOIR TOWN
Caledonian Rd.
Liverpool Rd.
Essex Rd.
ISLINGTON
N1
New North Rd.
HOXTON
Shepherdess Walk
Angel
Pentonville Rd.
HACKNEY
Cambridge Heath
Hackney Rd.
Roman Rd.
City Rd.
FINSBURY
Rosebery Ave.
Goswell Rd.
SHOREDITCH
Hackney Rd.
Bethnal Green
E2
St. John St.
Bethnal Green Rd.
BETHNAL GREEN
Farringdon Rd.
EC1
Old St.
Old St.
Great Eastern St.
Bethnal Green
CLERKENWELL
City Road
Shoreditch
Cambridge Heath Rd.
Clerkenwell Rd.
Whitechapel
Mile End Rd.
Chancery Lane
Hatton Gdn.
Barbican
Liverpool St. Station
Farringdon
The Barbican Centre
Liverpool St.
TOWER HAMLETS
High Holborn
London Wall
Moorgate
Whitechapel Rd.
HOLBORN
Holborn Viaduct
CITY (LONDON)
EC2
8
Bishopsgate
Aldgate East
STEPNEY
3
Bank of England
EC4
St. Paul's
Aldgate
WHITECHAPEL
Fleet St.
St. Paul's Cathedral
THE CITY
Bank
Leman St.
E1
Shadwell
Temple
Blackfriars
Mansion House
Cannon St.
Fenchurch St.
Fenchurch Station
Royal Mint
Cable St.
Shadwell
Victoria Embankment
Blackfriars Station
Cannon St.
EC3
Cannon St. Station
Monument
Tower Hill
Tower Gateway
SHADWELL
Waterloo Bridge
Thames
Blackfriars Bridge
12
Millennium Bridge
Southwark Bridge
2
13
London Bridge
Tower of London
Hungerford Bridge
BANKSIDE
London Bridge
WAPPING
Blackfriars Rd.
Southwark St.
Wapping
SOUTH BANK
Borough High St.
London Bridge Station
Tooley St.
Tower Bridge
York Rd.
Southwark
Waterloo
SOUTHWARK
Rotherhithe
Waterloo Station
Waterloo Rd.
Borough
BOROUGH
BERMONDSEY
SE1
Long Lane
ROTHERHITHE
Lambeth North
Borough Rd.
Great Dover St.
Tower Bridge Rd.
Lambeth Rd.
Elephant & Castle
ELEPHANT & CASTLE
New Kent Rd.
LAMBETH
Kennington Rd.
Old Kent Rd.
Walworth Rd.
SOUTHWARK
SE11
Kennington Ln.
LAMBETH
Park Rd.
WALWORTH
Kennington
SE17
KENNINGTON
The Oval (Surrey County Cricket Ground)
BURGESS PARK
Oval
Camberwell Rd.
Clapham Rd.
Camberwell New Rd.
SE5
CAMBERWELL
PECKHAM
London Transportation
Bank Underground Station
Camden Rd. British Rail Station
DLR Docklands Light Rail
Underground Lines
Bakerloo
Central
Circle
District
East London
Hammersmith & City
Jubilee
Metropolitan
Northern
Piccadilly
Victoria
Waterloo & City

You can explore the wonders of science, history, and nature at world-class museums, eat yourself to a bigger dress size at top-notch restaurants, marvel at just how much gold and jewelry fill the royal palaces and castles, and say you've "done" London. But to get to *know* London, you need to experience the special moments that reveal the city's true character. Here are some of the best:

❶ Take photos from the top of the London Eye. The top of this Ferris wheel is the best place to get a picture-perfect shot of London's far-reaching landscape. Any time is a good time for a ride but for a truly breathtaking photo opportunity book a "night flight" for when the sun starts sinking and the lights come on across the city. *See p 11, ❻.*

❷ Take an inter-art cruise aboard the Tate-to-Tate boat. Running between the sister galleries of Tate Britain and Tate Modern every 40 minutes, the boat allows you to instantly swap an eyeful of paintings and installations for views of some of the Thames' most iconic sights, including the London Eye and Big Ben. The boat itself is a work of art with a colorful spotted livery by Damien Hirst. *See p 19.*

❸ Get to know Londoners in their natural habitat with a pub crawl through the City. A trip to a traditional boozer can combine many interests, such as history (many pubs are housed in ancient buildings),

A pint at a traditional London pub.

dining, pub games, and, of course, there's a wide range of beers and wines to be sampled—just be sure to pace yourself. *See p 126.*

❹ Dig the music (classical or jazz) at the Late View at the V&A, held under the museum's thrilling Dale Chihuly glass chandelier on Friday evenings. Several of the renowned

A pod on the London Eye.

museum's galleries are open for exploring, and the relaxed atmosphere—helped by the open bar—makes for a leisurely and seductive visit. Pick up a ticket for one of the lectures that start at 7pm, and round off the night with a browse through the gift shop. *See p 33.*

5 **Dine next to a celebrity at the Wolseley,** but act unimpressed. Don't even think about autographs, cameras, or gaping at this Piccadilly hot spot, where the modern British cuisine is good and the clientele often stellar. Make lunch and dinner reservations in advance of your visit. Weekdays and nights are better than weekends to catch sight of a celeb, and remember that only Americans dine before 8pm. *See p 109.*

6 **Print a poster of your favorite masterpiece at the National Gallery.** The computers in the Sainsbury Wing offer virtual reconnaissance tours of this huge, world-renowned, treasure-packed museum and allow you to print high-quality posters of any painting in the gallery's collection in a variety of sizes. The database holds more than 2,000 works—it's a real kick to scroll through them. *See p 22,* **6**.

7 **Crisscross the scenic Serpentine in a pedal boat** on a sunny morning as ducks and geese wheel overhead. The little island on the north side is reputed to be local resident J. M. Barrie's inspiration for the Island of the Lost Boys in *Peter Pan.* Bring a camera. If you're not feeling too energetic, opt for a rowboat and let a companion do the work. *See p 90,* **6**.

8 **Drink champagne at the city's highest public vantage point, Vertigo 42.** Located on the top floor of Tower 42, one of the capital's tallest skyscrapers, the bar provides visitors with the best opportunity to observe the city from above, and to see the rival skyscrapers emerging across the skyline. *See p 121.*

9 **Haggle for a bargain at Portobello Road Market,** either at the open-air stalls or in the warrens of indoor arcades. You may get 10 to 15% off the asking price, which everyone involved knows is set just for that probability. Saturday's the big day for this famous antiques market, and part of the fun is sharing the street with seething crowds of bargain hunters and loiterers. *See p 85.*

10 **Listen to Big Ben strike the hour.** The bongs at midnight on December 31 will obviously get the biggest reaction, but this is a very London pleasure whatever the hour. It's the bell itself that's named Big Ben, though most assign that name to the whole clock tower. Although the bell has a crack in it and can't sound an E note, its chimed aria from Handel's *Messiah* is the undisputed aural symbol of London. *See p 10,* **2**.

11 **Ride down Hyde Park's Rotten Row on horseback** and you'll feel like a character out of a 19th-century English novel, as you pass joggers, in-line skaters, and cyclists.

Boats on the Serpentine lake, Hyde Park.

There's no better way to absorb the atmosphere of London's most popular park. Only skilled riders should let their horses try a canter; novices will still enjoy the experience at a walking gait. *See p 90,* **5**.

12 **Stand in the middle of the Thames on the Millennium Bridge,** which spans not just the river but also the centuries, with St. Paul's Cathedral on one side and the Tate Modern on the other. The views of the cityscape are impressive, especially at sunrise and sunset. *See p 13,* **9**.

13 **Become part of the play at Shakespeare's Globe Theatre** as one of the "groundlings" who stand in front of the stage, much as the rabble did during Shakespeare's time. You never know when the actors might mingle among you as they bellow out their lines. It's a truly Elizabethan experience, minus the pickpockets and the spitting. *See p 137.*

14 **Stuff yourself with a full afternoon tea** at the deluxe Goring hotel that rises to the task of impressing visitors with an array of sandwiches, scones with clotted cream, and

The maze at Hampton Court.

cakes—all washed down with a strong cuppa. Don't make dinner plans—you won't be hungry. *See p 104.*

15 **Explore the breadth of the old Empire at the British Museum,** where priceless treasures acquired from all parts of the globe—including the Rosetta Stone and the Elgin Marbles—testify to the power that Britain once exerted over the farthest reaches of the world, and give you insight into just how greedy its adventurers were. *See p 26.*

16 **Lose your way inside Hampton Court Palace's famous Hedge Maze,** with winding paths that cover nearly half a mile. When you manage to extricate yourself from its clutches, stroll through the many centuries of architectural styles featured at this stunning palace, which was the country home of many an English monarch, including Henry VIII. Don't neglect the gift shops. *See p 49,* **9**. ●

Ancient treasures at the British Museum.

1 The Best **Full-Day Tours**

The Best **in One Day**

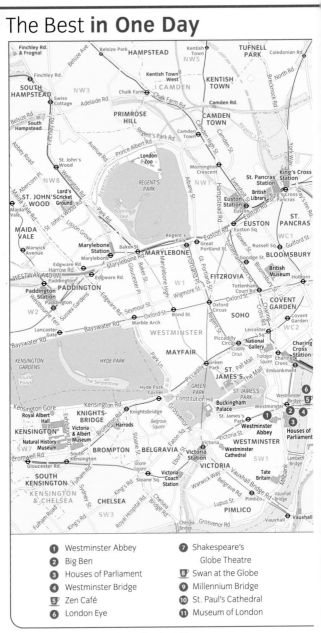

❶ Westminster Abbey	❼ Shakespeare's
❷ Big Ben	Globe Theatre
❸ Houses of Parliament	⑧ Swan at the Globe
❹ Westminster Bridge	❾ Millennium Bridge
⑤ Zen Café	❿ St. Paul's Cathedral
❻ London Eye	⓫ Museum of London

Previous page: St. Paul's dome from Millennium Bridge.

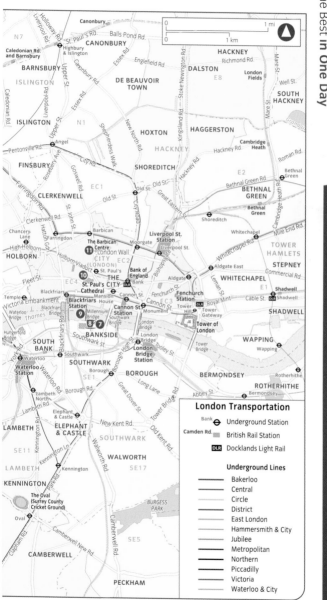

London Transportation

Bank ⊖ Underground Station

Camden Rd. ■ British Rail Station

DLR   Docklands Light Rail

Underground Lines

———— Bakerloo
———— Central
———— Circle
———— District
———— East London
———— Hammersmith & City
———— Jubilee
———— Metropolitan
———— Northern
———— Piccadilly
———— Victoria
———— Waterloo & City

This tour is of "Iconic London." You'll be visiting attractions, including Westminster Abbey and St. Paul's, that have been familiar to Londoners for hundreds of years, as well as more recent arrivals, such as the London Eye, and modern recreations of the past, such as Shakespeare's Globe. Total time: 1 day; total history covered: More than 1,000 years. START: **Tube to Westminster.**

Westminster Abbey.

❶ ★★★ Westminster Abbey.

The nearly 1,000-year-old abbey is one of the finest examples of medieval architecture in Europe. Like a giant shrine to the nation, it contains some 3,300 memorials to kings, nobles, and other great British figures from down the ages. William the Conqueror, Edward III, Mary Queen of Scots, Elizabeth I (whose death mask was the model for her tomb's figure), and Henry V, the hero of Agincourt, all have elaborately decorated sarcophagi. Don't miss the Gothic ceilings (reflected in a large mirror for close-up viewing), the stained glass in the Chapter House, and the elaborate carvings of the Henry VIII Chapel's choir stalls. And make your way to Poets' Corner, where you'll find

monuments to well-loved literary names such as Chaucer, Austen, and Dickens. ⏱ *1½ hr; arrive before 9:30am to avoid line-ups. 20 Dean's Yard.* ☎ *020/7222-5152. www. westminster-abbey.org. Adults £16, £13 seniors & students, £6 children 11–18, £32 family, free for children 10 & under. Free admission to services. Mon–Tues & Thurs–Fri 9:30am–4:30pm, Wed 9:30am–7pm, Sat 9:30am–2:30pm. Last admission 1 hr before closing. Closed Sun. Tube: Westminster.*

❷ ★ Big Ben.

The iconic clock tower at the eastern end of the Palace of Westminster has come to be known as Big Ben, although that appellation technically refers only to the tower's largest bell. The 14-tonne (13-ton) bell, installed in 1858, is believed to have been

Big Ben.

named after the rather portly commissioner of public works at the time—Sir Benjamin Hall. British residents can make the ascent up the tower's 334 spiral steps by special guided tour, but non-U.K. citizens must content themselves with a snapshot. ⏱ *5 min. Near St. Stephen's Entrance of Westminster Palace, Old Palace Yard. British citizens should contact their local M.P. to apply for permission to tour the clock tower.*

❸ ★ **Houses of Parliament.** The immense 3-hectare (7.4-acre) Palace of Westminster, a splendid example of Gothic Revival architecture, dates back to 1840 (the original palace was all but destroyed by fire in 1834). It's home to the 600-plus M.P.s (Members of Parliament, the elected representatives of the people) of the House of Commons and the 700-plus appointed members of the House of Lords (who scrutinize the decisions made in the Commons). You may observe debates for free from the Strangers' Galleries in both houses, but the long line-ups usually make this attraction better for a quick photo opportunity than a lengthy visit. The only exceptions are on Saturdays throughout the year and from Monday through Saturday during Parliament's summer recess, when the palace is open for guided tours. ⏱ *5 min. Old Palace Yard.* ☎ *020/7219-4272 House of Commons, 020/7219-3107 House of Lords. www. parliament.uk. Free admission. Mon–Tues 2:30–10:30pm, Wed 11:30am–7:30pm, Thurs 10:30am–6:30pm, Fri 9:30am–3pm. Closed Easter week. Guided tours (£15 adults, £6 children 16 & under) offered Sat 9:15am–4:30pm Aug–Sept (check website or call for exact tour times). Tube: Westminster.*

❹ **Westminster Bridge.** From the center of the bridge you can

The London Eye on the South Bank.

enjoy a sweeping view of the Houses of Parliament and Big Ben—one of the most familiar and beloved cityscapes in the world. ⏱ *10 min. Tube: Westminster.*

At County Hall you have a choice between a light snack of noodles at the ❺ ★ **Zen Café,** by the London Eye, or something a bit more fancy and filling at its sibling, **Zen China,** inside the building itself—the Peking Duck (£42 for two) comes highly recommended. *Westminster Bridge Rd.* ☎ *020/7261-1196. £–££.*

❻ ★★★ kids **London Eye.** The huge Ferris wheel that solemnly rotates one revolution per half-hour is already an icon of the city a mere decade since it opened, and is much loved by even the most hardened London traditionalist. You are encouraged to buy your timed ticket well in advance, which can end in disappointment if you get a gray

The ornate interior of St. Paul's Cathedral.

and rainy day—book yourself a "night flight" and you're guaranteed the twinkling lights of the city. Same-day tickets are sometimes available in the off-season. Show up 30 minutes before your scheduled departure time (15 if you have a Fast Track ticket). Don't forget your camera.

🕐 *1 hr, from lining up through half-hour ride. Book via the website for a 10% discount on the prices below. South Bank (at Westminster Bridge).* ☎ *0871/093-0123. www.londoneye. com. Adults £18.50, £15 seniors, £9.50 children 4–15, free for children 3 & under. Sept–Mar daily 10am–8:30pm, Apr–June & Sept 10am–9pm, July–Aug daily 10am–9:30pm. Closed bank holidays & 3 weeks in Jan. Tube: Westminster.*

❼ ★★ kids Shakespeare's Globe Theatre. Even if you don't have tickets to a play (p 137), the Globe is still a fascinating place to visit. It was rebuilt in painstaking detail on a parking lot near the site of the original theatre (and only those tools authentic to the period of the original were used in its construction). In the late 1500s/early 1600s Shakespeare's works were performed here to delight the nobility (who sat in the tiers) as well as

the rabble (who stood before the stage). You can choose either option when purchasing tickets, weighing comfort versus proximity to the stage. Changing displays at the on-site exhibition focus on topics such as the frost fairs of medieval London (back when the Thames would freeze solid and people would party on the river for days) or the juicy history of nearby Southwark, once a haven for prostitutes and thieves.

🕐 *1 hr. 21 New Globe Walk.* ☎ *020/7902-1400 (exhibition) or 020/7401-9919 (box office). www.shakespeares-globe.org. Admission to museum & exhibits: £11.50 adults, £10 seniors, £7 children 5–15, free for children 4 & under, £32 family (2 adults & 3 children). Daily 10am–5:30pm (closed during afternoon theatre matinees when tours of the remains*

The Millennium Bridge.

of the Rose Theatre are offered instead—call for schedules). *Tube: London Bridge.*

The **8** ★★ **kids Swan at the Globe** is a fine choice for a restorative break, and has a Thames-side view of London. The menu in the top-floor bar features English favorites, such as fish pie or sausage and mash, while the brasserie is a much fancier (and more expensive) affair. *21 Globe Walk (off Thames Path).* ☎ 020/7928-9444. £.

9 ★ **Millennium Bridge.** This sliver of a footbridge connecting Bankside to the City is a wonderful spot from which to take photos of the surrounding landmarks. When it first opened in 2000, it swayed and had to be shut down, but it has since been stabilized. ⏱ *10 min. Tube: Southwark or Blackfriars.*

10 ★★★ **kids St. Paul's Cathedral.** The dome of St. Paul's has been the defining icon of the London skyline since its creation after the Great Fire of 1666. Although it's no longer the city's tallest structure, no modern skyscraper (even the much admired "Gherkin") is held in such affection—or inspires the same awe— as Sir Christopher Wren's masterpiece. The cathedral was the culmination of Wren's unique and much-acclaimed fusion of classical (the exterior Greek-style columns) and baroque (the ornate interior decorations) architecture. The Whispering Gallery is a miracle of engineering, in which you can hear the murmurs of another person from across a large gallery. The 528 stairs to the Golden Gallery are demanding, but you'll be rewarded with a magnificent view not only of London but also of the interior of the cathedral. Wren—who is buried alongside many notable scientists and artists in the cathedral's

crypt—considered it his ultimate achievement. Guided tours (included in the admission price) are at 10:45 and 11:15am, 1:30 and 2pm. ⏱ *1½ hr. Ludgate Hill (at Paternoster Sq.).* ☎ *020/7236-8350. www.stpauls.co.uk. Adults £14.50, £13.50 seniors & students, £5.50 children 6–18. Mon–Sat 8:30am–4:30pm. Tube: St. Paul's.*

11 ★★ **kids Museum of London.** If it pertains to London's history, you'll find it here. Exhibits start at the prehistoric level and proceed to the 21st century, with stops at all the great and terrible moments in London's long life, including "Roman London," "Medieval London," and the Great Fire. Do not miss the ornate Lord Mayor's Coach, a 2.7-tonne (3-ton) gilt affair in which Cinderella would have felt right at home. ⏱ *1½ hr. London Wall.* ☎ *020/7001-9844. www.museum oflondon.org.uk. Free admission, except for temporary exhibits. Open daily 10am–6pm. Tube: St. Paul's.*

Armory on display at the Museum of London.

The Best **in Two Days**

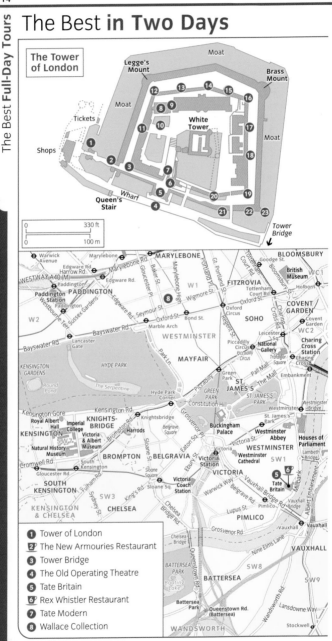

The Tower of London

0 ——— 330 ft
0 ——— 100 m

1 Tower of London
2 The New Armouries Restaurant
3 Tower Bridge
4 The Old Operating Theatre
5 Tate Britain
6 Rex Whistler Restaurant
7 Tate Modern
8 Wallace Collection

TOWER OF LONDON
Beauchamp Tower 11
Bell Tower 3
Bloody Tower 7
Bowyer Tower (torture chamber) 14
Brick Tower 15
Broad Arrow Tower 18
Byward Tower 2
Chapel Royal of St. Peter ad Vincula 8
Constable Tower 17
Cradle Tower 21
Develin Tower 23

Devereux Tower 12
Flint Tower 13
Jewel House (entrance) 9
Lanthorn Tower 20
Martin Tower 16
Middle Tower 1
St. Thomas's Tower 5
Salt Tower 19
Site of Scaffold 10
Traitors' Gate 4
Wakefield Tower 6
Well Tower 22

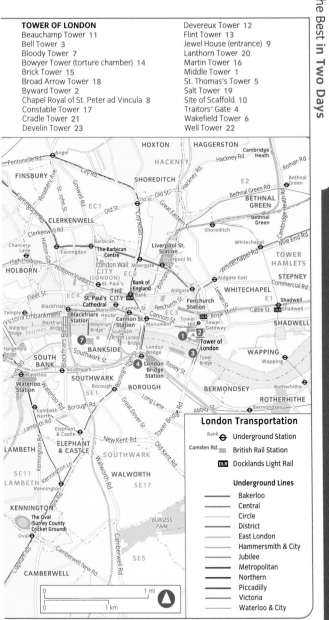

On the second day you'll delve into the capital's history, exploring the buildings, jewels, and ghosts that make up the Tower of London; British art at Tate Britain; and the gruesome horrors of the medical past at the Old Operating Theatre. You'll also experience the new at the Tate Modern and traverse the Thames by boat, now as always the watery heart of the city. START: **Tube to Tower Hill.**

❶ ★★★ kids Tower of London.

Begun by William the Conqueror in 1078, this fortress was added to by subsequent generations of kings and queens, and reflects the range of England's architectural styles over the past millennium. The Tower has a bloody past marked by power struggles, executions, and cruelty: The young nephews of Richard III were murdered here in 1483; two of Henry VIII's six wives (Anne Boleyn and Catherine Howard) were beheaded on Tower Green, as was the 9-day queen, Lady Jane Grey. Yeoman Warders (or "Beefeaters") give gore-filled talks all day long, and actors offer living history lessons as they wander about in period costumes. The Crown Jewels are the most popular sight, just edging out the Torture Exhibit; the two together represent the awful accoutrements of power (and have the longest line-ups). The haunted—and haunting—Tower will thrill students of history and entertain kids too. ⏱ *2 hr. Buy your tickets online & arrive when it opens to avoid the long line & save around 15% on the prices listed below. Tower Hill.* ☎ *0844/ 482-7777 (from the U.K.) or 020/ 3166-6000 (outside the U.K.). www. hrp.org.uk/TowerOfLondon/. Adults £19.80, £17.05 seniors, £10.45 children 5–15, free for children 4 & under, £55 family. Open Tues–Sat 9am– 5:30pm, Sun–Mon 10am–5:30pm, till 4:30pm Nov–Feb. Tube: Tower Hill.*

Beefeater at the Tower of London.

Buy sandwiches at ❷ ★★ **The New Armouries Restaurant** for an outdoor picnic, or settle in for a hot lunch of shepherd's pie, soup, or whatever you fancy. It's clean and pleasant though not hugely atmospheric. There are also snack shops scattered here and there around the Tower. *Inside the Tower of London.* ☎ *020/3166-6991. £.*

❸ ★★ kids Tower Bridge. This

picture-perfect bascule bridge—a term derived from the French for "seesaw"—has spanned the Thames since 1894. There's no denying the physical beauty of the neo-Gothic structure: Its skeleton of steel girders is clothed with ornate

Tower Ghosts

The Tower of London, said to be the most haunted spot in England, fairly overflows with supernatural manifestations of tormented souls.

The ghost of Queen Anne Boleyn (executed in 1536 on a trumped-up charge of treason after she'd failed to produce a male heir for Henry VIII) is the most frequently spotted. The tragic shades of the Little Princes—allegedly murdered by Richard III in 1483—have been spied in the Bloody Tower. Ghostly reenactments of the Tower Green beheading of the Countess of Salisbury—who was slowly hacked to death by her inept executioner on May 27 1541—have been seen on its anniversary. The screams of Guy Fawkes, who gave up his co-conspirators in the Gunpowder Plot under torture, reputedly still echo around the grounds.

Other spirits you may encounter (the no-nonsense Tower guards have had run-ins with them all) include Sir Walter Raleigh, Lady Jane Grey, and Henry VI.

masonry using Cornish granite and Portland stone designed to harmonize elegantly with the neighboring Tower of London. Its lower span opens and closes thanks to some heavy-duty hydraulics at least once a day (a board next to the bridge tells you when). You can find out more at the "Tower Bridge Experience" tour, when you can also ascend to the bridge's top level for a bird's-eye view of the Tower of London and the Thames, 43m (141 ft.) below. (Acrophobics need not apply.) ⏲ 1 hr. Tower Bridge. ☎ 020/7403-3761. www.tower bridge.org.uk. Adults £8, £5.60 seniors, £3.40 children 5–15, free for children 4 & under. Ticket office is on northwest side of bridge. Daily Apr–Sept 10am–6:30pm, Oct–Mar 9:30am–6pm. Tube: Tower Hill.

Tower Bridge.

4 ★★ **kids** **The Old Operating Theatre.** A wooden operating table where operations—usually amputations—were performed without anesthetic or antiseptic (leather restraints held the patient in place, while pain relief was provided by alcohol and the speed of the surgeon); an early pair of forceps, and other instruments of outdated medical practices will cure any complaints you may have about modern medicine. 🕐 *30 min. 9a St. Thomas's St.* ☎ *020//7188-2679. www.thegarret. org.uk. Adults £5.90, £4.90 seniors, £3.40 children 15 & under. Daily 10:30am–5pm. Tube: London Bridge.*

5 ★★ **kids** **Tate Britain.** Housed in a charming neoclassical building, which looks a bit like a miniature British Museum, Tate Britain opened in 1894 thanks to generous donations of money and art from sugar mogul Sir Henry Tate. Today, it boasts the country's finest collection of domestic art, covering the period from the 16th century to the present day, and has an unparalleled collection of works by renowned landscape artist J. M. W. Turner, who bequeathed most of his paintings to the museum. Other notable British artists whose works adorn the walls include satirist William Hogarth, illustrator William Blake, portraitist Thomas Gainsborough, and traditionalist Joshua Reynolds. 🕐 *1½ hr. Millbank.* ☎ *020/7887-8888. www. tate.org.uk/britain/. Free admission, except for temporary exhibits. Daily 10am–6pm. Tube: Pimlico.*

The Tate's own **6** ★★ **Rex Whistler Restaurant** serves tasty modern British cuisine in a cheery, mural-filled dining room. It's a great place for afternoon tea or, on weekends, for a superior "full English" breakfast (£9.25). *In the Tate Britain.* ☎ *020/7887-8825. ££.*

7 ★★★ **kids** **Tate Modern.** The world's most popular modern art gallery, this offshoot of Tate Britain is housed in the gargantuan shell of a converted 1940s' brick power station. Through the main entrance, you enter a vast space, the Turbine Hall, where a succession of temporary exhibitions is held—the bigger and more ambitious, the better. Highlights have included 100 million ceramic sunflower seeds covering the floor (Ai Weiwei) and a maze made out of 14,000 polyethylene boxes (Rachel Whiteread). Spread over three levels, the permanent collection encompasses a great body of modern art dating from 1900 to now. It covers all the big hitters, including Matisse, Rothko, Pollock, Picasso, Dalí, Duchamp, and Warhol, and is arranged according to movements—surrealism, minimalism, cubism, expressionism, and so on. Free themed 45-minute guided tours of the collection are at 11am, noon, 2, and 3pm. A new gallery extension, taking the form of an asymmetrical, brick-and-glass pyramid, is due to open in 2012. 🕐 *1½ hr. Multimedia guides are available from the info*

Tate Britain.

The Turbine Hall, Tate Modern.

desks on levels 2 & 3 (£3.50). Bankside. ☎ 020/7887-8888. www.tate. org.uk/modern/. *Free admission, except for temporary exhibits. Daily 10am–6pm. Tube: Southwark, St. Paul's, or London Bridge.*

8 ★★ kids Wallace Collection. This collection offers an astonishing glimpse into the buying power of the English gentry following the French Revolution, when important art and furnishings were made homeless by the guillotine. In 1897, Lady Wallace left this entire mansion and its contents to the nation on the condition that they be kept intact, without additions or subtractions. The paintings are outstanding, with works by Titian, Gainsborough, Rembrandt, and Hals (including his famous *Laughing Cavalier*), and the collection also includes Sèvres porcelain, 18th-century French decorative art, and an array of European and Asian armaments that are works of art in their own right. ⏱ *1 hr. Hertford House, Manchester Sq. ☎ 020/7563-9500. www.wallace collection.org. Free admission. Daily 10am–5pm. Take a free guided tour at 11am Mon–Fri, 11:30am Wed & Sat, and 3pm Sun. Tube: Bond St.*

Sailing the Tate Boat

The Tate boat ferry service between the two Tate galleries on opposite banks of the Thames is one of London's more useful tourist creations. The same people who built the London Eye designed the ferry's dramatic Millbank Pier, and the colorful catamaran was decorated by the once *enfant terrible* of the British art scene, Damian Hirst. The 18-minute ride stops off en route at the London Eye (p 11, ⑥), and makes a convenient and scenic way to get from one to the other.

Alas, it's not free. One-way ferry tickets cost £5 adults, £2.50 kids 5 to 15, free for kids 4 and under. If you have a London Travelcard (p 161), you get a good discount. Tickets can be bought online or at the Tate Britain or Tate Modern. The boat runs daily every 40 minutes (more often in high season) between 10am and 6pm. For precise boat times, call ☎ 020/7887-8888 or check www.tate.org.uk/tatetotate.

The Best **in Three Days**

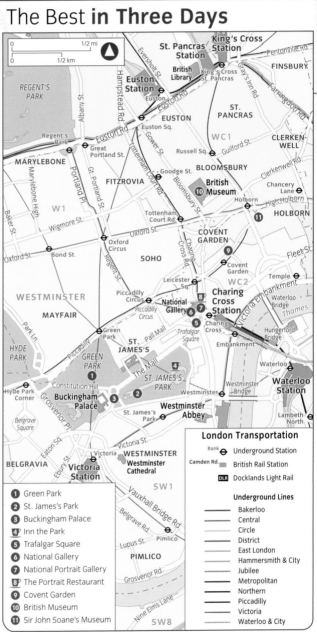

1 Green Park
2 St. James's Park
3 Buckingham Palace
4 Inn the Park
5 Trafalgar Square
6 National Gallery
7 National Portrait Gallery
8 The Portrait Restaurant
9 Covent Garden
10 British Museum
11 Sir John Soane's Museum

London Transportation

Bank	Underground Station
Camden Rd.	British Rail Station
DLR	Docklands Light Rail

Underground Lines

Bakerloo
Central
Circle
District
East London
Hammersmith & City
Jubilee
Metropolitan
Northern
Piccadilly
Victoria
Waterloo & City

The tour begins with some of London's most utterly British attractions—the sweeping royal parks and the pomp and ceremony of the Changing of the Guard—and finishes with the gloriously elegant clutter of Sir John Soane's Museum. In between are the National Gallery and perhaps the finest museum of human civilization, the British Museum. START: **Tube to Green Park.**

❶ ★ **kids** **Green Park.** London's royal parks are often busy affairs, filled with flowerbeds, statues, ponds, playgrounds, and more, but all you'll find here are acres of rolling green lawns and tall shady trees, plus, in summer, scores of local workers sunning their lunch hours away either on the grass or on the stripy deckchairs (£1.50) that represent the park's one formal facility. Founded in 1660 in order to allow Charles II to travel between St. James's Park and Hyde Park without leaving royal soil, the park's pared-down nature supposedly dates from the time the queen caught Charles giving flowers from the park to another woman. In a rage, she had all the flowerbeds torn up. ⏱ *15 min. Tube: Green Park.*

❷ ★★ **kids** **St. James's Park.** Southeast of Green Park, this is arguably London's prettiest park. It's certainly difficult to believe that this was, until the 18th century, the center of a notorious scene, where prostitutes conducted their business and drunken rakes took unsteady aim at dueling opponents. It's now very respectable, with a wildfowl pond, weeping willows, and numerous flowerbeds. ⏱ *30 min.*

❸ ★ **Buckingham Palace.** "Buck House," the queen's famous abode in London (if the yellow-and-red Royal standard is flying, it means she's home), is the setting for the pageantry of the **Changing of the Guard,** a London tradition that attracts more people than it

View over the pond at St. James's Park.

Trafalgar Square.

warrants. A better place to see all the queen's horses and all the queen's men in action is at Horse Guards Parade (p 71, ❸). But if you're determined to watch the guards change here, arrive a half-hour early to get a seat by the statue of Victoria; it offers a reasonably good view. The ceremony begins at 11:30am sharp every day between May and July, and on alternate days for the rest of the year—in theory, anyway; it's often canceled in bad weather. 🕑 *30 min. See p 35,* ❶.

At the northeast end of St. James's Park is ❹ ★★ kids **Inn the Park.** Skip the overpriced restaurant; the same chefs supply the cafeteria-style eatery, which features picturesque views of the London Eye and Whitehall. *In St. James's Park (by Pall Mall).* ☎ *020/7451-9999. £.*

❺ kids **Trafalgar Square.** Where a visit to this square once involved battling traffic and dodging pigeons,

a part-pedestrianization and a ban on pigeon-feeding means that it is now once again possible to appreciate the fine surroundings. Bordering the square are the National Gallery on the northern side, St. Martin-in-the-Fields to the east, and, in the northwest corner, the "Fourth Plinth," which hosts temporary art installations. Towering above them is a pillar topped with a statue of Britain's most revered naval hero, Horatio, Viscount Nelson. The square is the scene of rallies, demonstrations, and celebrations. 🕑 *15 min.*

❻ ★★★ kids **National Gallery.** This outstanding art museum dominating the north side of Trafalgar Square sits roughly where the stables of King Henry VIII used to be. Founded in 1832 with a collection of 38 paintings bought by the British government, the National is now home to some 2,300 works representing the development of western European painting from 1250 to 1900.

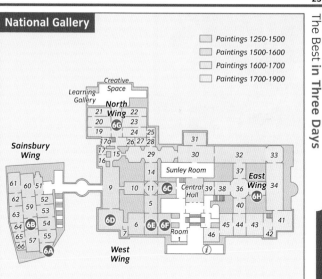

National Gallery

Paintings 1250-1500
Paintings 1500-1600
Paintings 1600-1700
Paintings 1700-1900

Start in the **6A** ★★★ **Sainsbury Wing's Room 56**, where you'll find early European works, including Van Eyck's haunting *The Arnolfini Portrait*. Note the words inscribed over the mirror: JAN VAN EYCK WAS HERE/1434. For a contrast in mood, go to **6B Room 58** for Botticelli's voluptuous *Venus and Mars*. The **6C West Wing's Room 12** holds Titian's *Bacchus and Ariadne,* its colors still vibrant after 500 years; in **6D Room 8** is an ethereal Raphael painting of *The Madonna of the Pinks* (1506) as well as a couple of Michelangelos. Holbein's *Ambassadors* is in **6E Room 4**; the skull in the foreground looks distorted unless you look at it from a side angle. Pay your respects to da Vinci in **6F Room 2,** and then leave the Renaissance for the **6G North Wing** and Dutch, French, and Spanish masterpieces from 1600 to 1800, including Rembrandt's self-portrait at the age of 34 in Room 24. Finish at the **6H East Wing** and the works of Impressionists van Gogh (including his *Sunflowers* in Room 45 just inside the main entrance), Monet, and Renoir, among others. ⏱ *1½ hr. Trafalgar Sq.* ☎ *020/7747- 2285. www. nationalgallery.org.uk. Free admission, except for temporary exhibits. Daily 10am–6pm, till 9pm Fri. Tube: Charing Cross or Leicester Sq.*

7 ★★ kids **National Portrait Gallery.** Adjacent to the National Gallery, the NPG is the best place to put faces to the names of those who have shaped Britain politically, socially, and culturally. The gallery's 10,000-plus portraits take in everyone from King Harold II (b. 1022),

A cafe within Covent Garden market.

Henry VIII, Shakespeare, and Charles Dickens, to modern figures such as David Bowie and Princess Diana. Start at the top, where the earliest works are located. ⏲ *1 hr. 2 St. Martin's Lane.* ☎ *020/7306-0055. www. npg.org.uk. Free admission, except for temporary exhibits. Sat–Wed 10am–6pm, Thurs–Fri 10am–9pm. Tube: Charing Cross or Leicester Sq.*

8 ★★★ **The Portrait Restaurant,** on the top floor of the NPG, commands spectacular views over Trafalgar Square. It's open throughout the day and for dinner Thursday to Saturday, and serves a mean afternoon tea. For cheaper snacks try the Portrait Café. *National Portrait Gallery, 2 St. Martin's Lane.* ☎ *020/7312-2490. ££.*

9 ★★★ kids **Covent Garden.** The great fruit and vegetable market that used to form this area's centerpiece moved out in the early 1970s but the glorious 19th-century

market buildings remain. **Jubilee Market,** with inexpensive whatnots, is set on the southern side of the arcade; at the western end you'll find antiques, crafts, and flea market goods. A motley collection of jugglers and physical comedians perform on the piazza, while in the main market building you may experience an operatic performance given by professionals from the neoclassical **Royal Opera House,** which faces the arcade. ⏲ *30 min. Tube: Covent Garden.*

10 ★★★ kids **British Museum.** You could spend days exploring this world-renowned museum, but an hour or so is enough to get a flavor of what it has to offer. If you're visiting on a Friday, you can stay till 8:30pm and enjoy a range of additional events, including films and lectures. ⏲ *1 hr. See tour p 26.*

11 ★★ **Sir John Soane's Museum.** The distinguished British architect Sir John Soane (1753–1837) was also an avid collector. The bulk of this collection was amassed at the height of empire, when antiquities could be removed from their country of origin and displayed casually in one's home. Ancient tablets, sculptures, paintings (including William Hogarth's celebrated *Rake's Progress*), architectural models, and even an Egyptian sarcophagus are strewn around in no particular order, and the haphazardness of the display is part of the museum's charm. On the first Tuesday evening of each month, visitors can explore the museum by candlelight. ⏲ *1 hr. 13 Lincoln's Inn Fields.* ☎ *020/7405-2107. www. soane.org. Free admission. Tues–Sat 10am–5pm, late night first Tues of month 6–9pm. Tube: Holborn.* ●

The British Museum

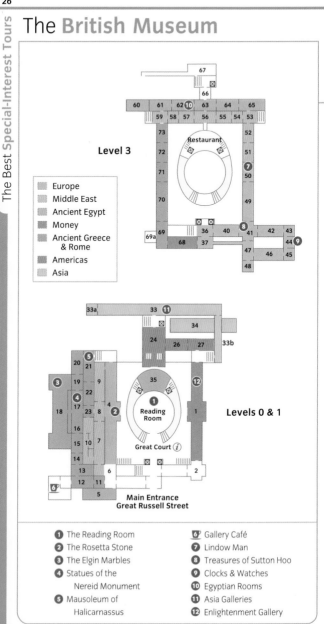

Level 3

67
66
60 61 62 ⑩ 63 64 65
59 58 57 56 55 54 53
73
Restaurant
72 52
71 51
⑦
70 50
49

Europe
Middle East
Ancient Egypt
Money
Ancient Greece & Rome
Americas
Asia

69a 69 36 40 41 42 43
68 37 ⑧ 44 ⑨
47 46 45
48

33a 33 ⑪
34
24 33b
26 27

20 21 ⑤
⑶ 19 9
22 35 ⑫
⑷ 17 23 8 ② 4 1
18 16
15 10 7 **Levels 0 & 1**
14
⑹ 13 6
12 11 2
5
**Main Entrance
Great Russell Street**

① Reading Room
Great Court ⓘ

① The Reading Room
② The Rosetta Stone
③ The Elgin Marbles
④ Statues of the
   Nereid Monument
⑤ Mausoleum of
   Halicarnassus

⑹ Gallery Café
⑦ Lindow Man
⑧ Treasures of Sutton Hoo
⑨ Clocks & Watches
⑩ Egyptian Rooms
⑪ Asia Galleries
⑫ Enlightenment Gallery

Previous page: Changing of the Guard at Buckingham Palace.

The British Museum, started with a donation by the royal physician and collector Sir Hans Sloane in 1753, opened at a time when the expansion of the British Empire ensured that its collection would be as eclectic as it was priceless. Note the frieze above the entrance—it signifies the museum's intention to encompass all the branches of science and art. START: **Tube to Holborn.**

❶ ★★ The Reading Room.

Located at the center of the Great Court, beneath the museum's crazy-paving-style glass roof, this was once the home of the British Library (p 40, ❺)—now moved to more spacious, if rather less elegant, premises in Euston. It was restored to its 1857 grandeur for the millennium, and today provides a sophisticated setting for temporary exhibitions (entrance fees usually apply). Note the list of authors on either side of the entrance doors, including Dickens, Marx, Tennyson, Kipling, and Darwin, who all once sat within composing some of literature's finest works. ⏲ *15 min.*

❷ ★★★ The Rosetta Stone.

One of the museum's most highly prized artifacts is an ancient text engraved on a tablet in three scripts (hieroglyphic, demotic, and Greek) that celebrates the virtues of 13-year-old pharaoh Ptolemy V, who lived in 196 B.C. The tablet was found in 1799 by Napoleon's troops and handed over to the British Army as part of the Alexandria Treaty of 1802. The text was deciphered in 1822, a breakthrough that allowed scholars to finally decode ancient Middle Eastern hieroglyphics. *Room 4.* ⏲ *5 min.*

❸ ★★★ The Elgin Marbles.

The Greek government has been fighting for 2 centuries to get these sculptures—taken from the Parthenon by Lord Elgin in 1805—returned to Athens. The B.M. argues that it has provided a safe home for these carvings (including 75m/246 ft. of the original temple frieze), which would otherwise have been chipped away by vandals or degraded by remaining in the open

The Reading Room under the roof of the Great Court.

air. The marbles may yet be returned to the Parthenon (which would probably prove a disastrous precedent for the museum, filled as it is with the booty of the world), but don't expect this to happen anytime soon. *Room 18.* ⏱ *20 min.*

④ ★ **Statues of the Nereid Monument.** This 4th-century-B.C. Lykian tomb from southwest Turkey arrived at the museum with the Elgin Marbles in 1816, and its lifelike statuary is almost surreal. Even without their heads, the Nereids (daughters of the sea god Nereus) look as graceful as the ocean waves they are meant to personify. *Room 17.* ⏱ *5 min.*

⑤ ★★ **Mausoleum of Halicarnassus.** These are the remains of one of the Seven Wonders of the Ancient World—the breathtaking Ionian Greek tomb built for King Maussollos, from whose name the word "mausoleum" is derived. The huge tomb, some 40m (130 ft.) high, remained undisturbed from 351 B.C. to medieval times, when it was damaged by an earthquake. In 1494, Crusaders used its stones to fortify a castle; in 1846, sections of the tomb's frieze were found at the castle and given to the B.M. Subsequent excavations turned up the remarkably lifelike horse sculpture and the series of lounging figures. *Room 21.* ⏱ *15 min.*

The excellent ⑥ ★★ **kids** **Gallery Café** is a relaxed, cafeteria-style eatery decorated with the 1801 casts of the Elgin Marbles. The hot meals, sandwiches, and desserts are all reasonably priced. *Off Room 12.* ☎ *020/7323-8990. £.*

⑦ ★★ **kids** **Lindow Man.** Don't miss the leathery cadaver of the "Bog Man" (aka "Pete Marsh"), found in 1984 preserved in a peat bog in Cheshire, where he had lain for nearly 2,000 years. The poor man had been struck on the head, garroted, knifed, and then put head first into the bog. His excessive wounds suggest he died in a sacrificial ritual. *End of Room 50, on your right.* ⏱ *5 min.*

⑧ ★★★ **Treasures of Sutton Hoo.** Sutton Hoo was a burial ground of the early Anglo-Saxons

Practical Matters—The British Museum

The British Museum (☎ 020/7323-8299; www.britishmuseum.org) is located on Great Russell Street. Take the Tube to Tottenham Court Road, Russell Square, or Holborn.

Admission is free (donations appreciated), except to temporary exhibitions. The museum is open daily from 10am to 5:30pm; on Friday, select galleries remain open until 8:30pm when special events are laid on. A variety of specialty tours range from self-operated multimedia guides (£5) to free, 40-minute introductory "Eyeopener" tours; check the website for details or inquire at the Information Desk in the museum's Great Court. The museum's website provides information on thousands of objects in the collection.

(including one royal, who literally went down with his 30m (98-ft.) oak ship). When this tomb was excavated in 1939, previous beliefs about the inferior arts and crafts of England's Dark Age (around A.D. 625) were confounded, as well-designed musical instruments, glassware, and armor (including the iconic Sutton Hoo helmet) were uncovered. *Room 41.* ⏱ *15 min.*

9 ★★ **Clocks & Watches.** The museum's outstanding collection of timepieces dating from the Middle Ages to the present day features the mind-blowing mechanical Galleon (or "Nef") Clock, which used to roll along a table announcing dinnertime to guests. Built (in 1585 in Germany) to resemble a medieval ship, the gilt-copper marvel played music, beat drums, and even fired tiny cannons. *Room 39.* ⏱ *20 min.*

10 ★★★ **kids Egyptian Rooms.** Room 62 is dedicated to death and the afterlife and is filled with coffins, sarcophagi, funerary objects, and, of course, mummies. There's even a mummified cat, and it's said that the ghost of one of these 3,000-year-old bandaged corpses still haunts these rooms. ⏱ *30 min.*

11 ★★ **Asia Galleries.** Room 33 is an oasis of calm and includes meditating Buddhas and the Dancing Shiva—a bronze sculpture depicting one of India's most famous icons. The intricate frieze of the **Great Stupa** (Room 33a), carved in India in the 3rd century B.C., so closely resembles the Elgin Marbles that you'll wonder about the artistic zeitgeist that seemed to pass unaided through borders and cultures. There are statues of bodhisattvas, Buddhist archetypes, in

Artist sketching in the Egyptian Rooms.

every medium—from porcelain to metal. ⏱ *20 min.*

12 ★ **Enlightenment Gallery.** "Discovering the World in the 18th Century" is the subtitle of this permanent exhibit. Designed for George III by Sir Robert Smirke, the room is regarded as the finest and largest neoclassical interior hall in London. You'll be reaching for your pince-nez and quill pen as you marvel at the polished mahogany bookshelves stuffed with rare books. Display cases are filled with some 5,000 items that demonstrate the far-reaching, eclectic passions of the 18th-century Enlightenment scholar—the kind of person who made the British Museum possible. ⏱ *30 min.*

Victoria & Albert Museum

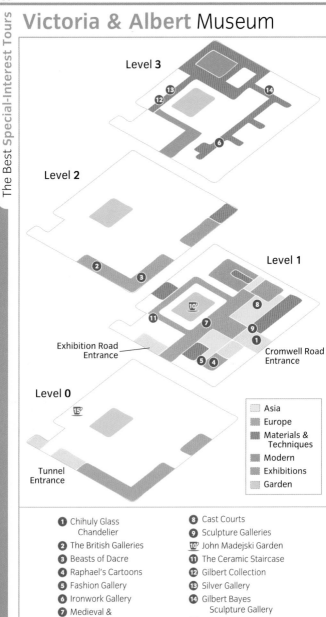

Level **3**

Level **2**

Level **1**

Exhibition Road
Entrance

Cromwell Road
Entrance

Level **0**

Tunnel
Entrance

Asia	
Europe	
Materials & Techniques	
Modern	
Exhibitions	
Garden	

1 Chihuly Glass
   Chandelier
2 The British Galleries
3 Beasts of Dacre
4 Raphael's Cartoons
5 Fashion Gallery
6 Ironwork Gallery
7 Medieval &
   Renaissance Galleries

8 Cast Courts
9 Sculpture Galleries
10 John Madejski Garden
11 The Ceramic Staircase
12 Gilbert Collection
13 Silver Gallery
14 Gilbert Bayes
   Sculpture Gallery
15 V&A Café

This museum's 8 miles of galleries are resplendent with the world's greatest collection of decorative arts. Opened in 1852 by Prince Albert, this glittering treasure-trove, known as the V&A, is made up of millions of pieces of priceless arts and crafts. A massive refurbishment continues to polish its glorious displays. START: **Tube to South Kensington.**

❶ ★★★ Chihuly Glass Chandelier.
Renowned glass artist Dale Chihuly created this serpentine green-and-blue masterpiece (in the main entrance) specifically for the V&A in 2001, when an exhibition of his work was staged in the museum's outdoor courtyard. It's 8m (26 ft.) long, and made up of thousands of exquisite hand-blown glass baubles. Despite its airy effect, it weighs 1.7 metric tons (3,750 pounds). *Foyer.* ⏱ *3 min.*

❷ ★★★ kids The British Galleries.
This stellar example of 21st-century curatorship features some of England's greatest cultural treasures. The big draw is the **Great Bed of Ware** (Room 57), a masterpiece of woodcarving mentioned in Shakespeare's *Twelfth Night.* Built in around 1590 as a sales gimmick for an inn, the bed is now covered in I WAS HERE graffiti and wax seals left by centuries of visitors. Another highlight is the *Portrait of Margaret Laton* (Room 56); the painting of the early-17th-century noblewoman is rather ordinary, but the fine jacket embroidered with silver thread and colored silks displayed alongside it is the very one worn in the portrait. ⏱ *1 hr.*

❸ ★★ Beasts of Dacre.
These four carved heraldic animals (gryphon, bull, dolphin, and ram) were carved for the Dacres, one of northern England's most important families, in 1520. The wooden figures survived a fire in 1844, only to be restored in a rather gaudy, Victorian carousel style. *Stairway C.* ⏱ *5 min.*

❹ ★★★ Raphael's Cartoons.
Dating back to 1521, these immense and expertly rendered drawings ("cartoon" is derived from the Italian word for a large piece of paper, *cartone*) were used by the artist Raphael to plot a set of tapestries originally intended to hang in the Sistine Chapel. *Room 48a.* ⏱ *15 min.*

❺ ★★ kids Fashion Gallery.
One of the world's largest collections of fashionable dresses will reopen in 2012 following a 2-year refurbishment, boasting everything from a ludicrous 18th-century 1.2m-(4-ft.) wide skirt to vertiginous platform shoes by Vivienne Westwood. *Room 40.* ⏱ *25 min.*

Sixties dress in the Fashion Gallery.

6 ★★ **Ironwork Gallery.** Past all the curlicued gates and nostalgic displays of cookie tins lining the museum's longest gallery, you'll find the stupendous **Hereford Screen,** a masterpiece of Victorian ironwork designed by the same man who devised the Albert Memorial (p 36, **6**). Check out the bird's-eye view of the foyer's chandelier. *Room 114.* ⏱ *20 min.*

7 ★★★ **Medieval & Renaissance Galleries.** These galleries are spread over three floors (0, 1, and 2) and aim to provide a complete overview of the progress of European art and culture from A.D. 300 to 1600; no mean ambition. The galleries comprise a mélange of tapestries, stained glass, statuary, glass, and metalwork. Notable items include Sir Paul Pindar's house, a rare wooden facade from a pre-Great Fire of London building and, in Room 64, a densely packed notebook bursting with ideas from the mind of Leonardo da Vinci. *Rooms 21–25.* ⏱ *30 min.*

8 ★★★ **kids Cast Courts.** These two popular rooms contain plaster-cast copies of some of the most famous European sculptures throughout history, including Trajan's Column (in two giant pieces), a version of Michelangelo's iconic *David* (whose nudity so shocked Queen Victoria that she had a fig leaf made for it—it's now displayed behind the statue), and a copy of Ghiberti's famous bronze doors for Florence's Baptistery. *Rooms 46a (46b will reopen in 2012).* ⏱ *20 min.*

9 ★★ **Sculpture Galleries.** British garden and funerary sculptures from the 18th century fill rooms 22 to 24, and since 2010 these have been joined by another couple of galleries (rooms 26 and 27) of religious sculptures. Produced in Western Europe between 1300 and 1600, these wooden figures were vividly painted, giving them an almost hyper-real appearance. ⏱ *20 min.*

For a quick outdoor snack, grab a table or recline on the lush lawns of the **10** **kids John Madejski Garden.** The water jets are great fun for kids, and on a sunny day you may not want to go back into the museum. *Inner Courtyard. Open summer only. £.*

The Sculpture Galleries.

The V&A—Practical Matters

The Victoria & Albert Museum (☎ 020/7942-2000; www.vam.ac.uk) is located on Cromwell Road, off Exhibition Road. Take the Tube to South Kensington and follow the signs to the museum.

Admission is free, except to special exhibitions. The museum is open daily from 10am to 5:45pm. On Friday, the V&A stays open until 10pm for the Late View, when live music, guided tours, and lectures are offered (it's best for adults). On weekends and school breaks, there are special activities for kids of all ages.

⓫ ★★ The Ceramic Staircase. The V&A's first director, Henry Cole, designed these stairs, intending to doll up all the museum's staircases in this ceramics-gone-mad style. For better or worse, when costs spiraled out of control in 1870 the project was quietly dropped. *Staircase I.* 🕐 *10 min.*

⓬ ★★ Gilbert Collection. This shimmering array of gold jewelry, silvery statuary, mosaics, enamel portraits, and other historic *objets d'art* was put together by the British-born businessman Sir Arthur Gilbert and donated to the nation in 1996. The stars of the show are the almost ridiculously opulent jewel-encrusted 18th-century snuffboxes. *Rooms 70–73.* 🕐 *25 min.*

⓭ ★★ Silver Gallery. This hall displays a jaw-dropping array of more than 10,000 silver objects from the past 600 years, ranging from baby rattles and candelabras to bath-size punch bowls. Highlights include a 15th-century German reliquary depicting an arrow-pierced St. Sebastian, Elizabethan gambling counters, and ornate 17th-century Swedish drinking tankards. Check out the interactive educational displays to learn some secrets of silver smithery. *Rooms 65–70a.* 🕐 *25 min.*

⓮ ★★ Gilbert Bayes Sculpture Gallery. This narrow gallery takes a look at the craft of sculpture, showing each stage of the creative process with pieces selected from different eras to showcase the various techniques and materials (including stone, bronze, and ivory) used by sculptors. It also gives you a treetop view of the Cast Courts. *Room 111.* 🕐 *20 min.*

The splendid **⓯ V&A Café** stands next to the V&A's original 19th-century refreshment rooms (the world's first museum restaurant) and is overlooked by stained glass and ornate ceramics and tiles. The food includes traditional hot English fare, plus sandwiches and salads. *Ground Level. £.*

Royal London

1 Buckingham Palace
2 Queen's Gallery
3 Palace Lounge
4 Royal Mews
5 Clarence House
6 Albert Memorial
7 Kensington Palace

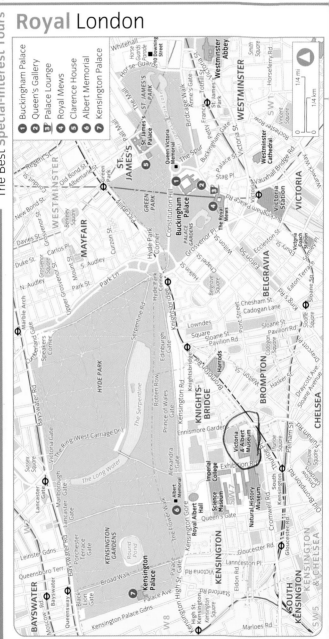

The various justifications for keeping the institution of the British monarchy inevitably come down to the entertainment of tourists, who can't get enough of the wealth, history, and gossip that have always defined royalty. This full-day tour serves up some of the city's royal highlights and offers a glimpse into the London lives of royals, past and present. START: **Tube to Green Park.**

1 ★ **Buckingham Palace.** The tour starts at the top with Buckingham Palace, the main residence of Queen Elizabeth II. The palace was originally built for the Duke of Buckingham and sold to King George III (who needed the room for his 15 children) in 1761. George IV had it remodeled by famed architect John Nash in the 1820s. For most of the year, you'll have to content yourself with views through the railings of its rather boxy exterior and the Changing of the Guard (p 21, **3**). However, for 10 weeks from late July to September, when the queen is elsewhere, a few of the palace's lavish 500 plus rooms are opened up for guided tours, including the State Room and Throne Room. You can also take a short tour of the garden. The palace has an aloofness that

makes it difficult to love, but still provides a fascinating glimpse inside one of the gilded cages of British royalty. Book the earliest timed tour possible via the website to avoid the worst of the lines. *Buckingham Palace Rd.* ☎ *020/7766-7300. www.royalcollection.org.uk. Admission (includes self-guided audio tour) £17.50 adults, £16 over 60, £10 children 5–16, £46 family. Late July–Sept daily 9:45am–6:30pm (last admission 3:45pm). Changing of the Guard: daily 11am May–July; 11am alternate days Aug–Apr. Tube: Green Park.*

2 ★★ **Queen's Gallery.** This well-curated museum answers the question of how one furnishes and decorates a palace or two. Priceless treasures from the queen's private

Changing of the Guard at Buckingham Palace.

collection of paintings, jewelry, furniture, and bibelots are displayed in sumptuous Georgian-style surroundings. The exhibits rotate (the queen's holdings include, among other items, 10,000 Old Masters and enough *objets d'art* to fill several palaces—which they do when they aren't here), but whatever is on display will be top-notch. You'll also find the city's best gift shop for royalty-related items, both cheap and expensive. ⏱ 1½ hr. *Buckingham Palace Road.* ☎ 020/7766-7301. *www.royalcollection.org.uk. Timed tickets necessary in summer. Admission £9 adults, £8.20 seniors, £4.50 children 5–16, free for children 4 & under. Daily 10am–5:30pm (last admission 4:30pm). Tube: Victoria or Green Park.*

Overlooking the entrance to the Royal Mews is the ③ **Palace Lounge,** an atmospheric spot to take traditional afternoon tea (£27.50 per person) or a light meal. You may get a glimpse of deliveries being made to Buckingham Palace in old-fashioned wagons. *In the Rubens at the Palace, 39 Buckingham Palace Rd.* ☎ 020/7834-6600. ££.

④ ★ **kids Royal Mews.** This oddly affecting royal experience is a great diversion if you're waiting for your timed entry to Buckingham Palace. Even if you're not into horses, you'll be fascinated by this peek into the lives of the queen's privileged equines. The stalls at this working stable are roomy, the tack is pristine, and the ceremonial carriages (including the ornate Gold State Coach and the coach that both princesses Diana and Catherine rode in after their weddings to their respective princes) are eye-popping. A small exhibit tells you about the role the queen's horses

have played in the past and present; old sepia-toned pictures show various royals and their four-footed friends. ⏱ 45 min. *Buckingham Gate.* ☎ 020/7766-7302. *www.royalcollection.org.uk. Adults £8, £7.25 seniors, £5 children 5–16, free for children 4 & under, £21.25 family. Apr–Oct daily 10am–5pm, Nov–Dec Mon–Sat 10am–4pm, Jan–Mar Mon–Fri 11am–4pm. Tube: Victoria or Green Park.*

⑤ ★ **Clarence House.** The list of former inhabitants of this rather staid mansion reads like a who's who of recent royals. It was designed in the 1820s by John Nash, the Royal Family's then favorite architect, for the Duke of Clarence, who continued residing there during his brief 7-year reign as William IV. In 1947 it was home to Princess Elizabeth following her marriage to Prince Philip. Before she succeeded to the throne she had given way to her mother, the "Queen Mother," who lived here until her death in 2002. Today, it's the official residence of Prince Charles and the Duchess of Cornwall, who are responsible for its current tastefully jumbled interior. In August visitors can take a guided tour of five staterooms, where a good deal of the queen's collection of art and furniture is displayed. ⏱ 1 hr. *Stable Yard Gate.* ☎ 020/7766-7303. *www.royalcollection.org.uk. Adults £8.50, £4.50 children 5–16, free for children 4 & under. Aug (dates subject to change; call first) daily 10am–5:30pm. Tube: Green Park or St. James's Park.*

⑥ ★ **kids Albert Memorial.** An inconsolable Queen Victoria spent an obscene amount of public money on this 55m-tall (180-ft.) gaudy shrine to her husband, Albert, who died of typhoid fever in 1861. The project (completed in 1876) didn't go down too well with her ministers, but Victoria was not a woman to whom one said no. The excessively ornate mass of gilt, marble, statuary, and mosaics set in Kensington Gardens stands in all its dubious glory across the street from the equally fabulous (and somewhat more useful) Albert Hall. The book Albert is holding is a catalogue from the Great Exhibition of which he was patron, and which formed the basis for the great museums of South Kensington. ⏱ *20 min. Kensington Gardens (west of Exhibition Rd.). Free admission. Daily dawn–dusk. Tube: High St. Kensington.*

❼ ★★★ kids Kensington Palace. A royal palace since the late 17th century, when the original Jacobean mansion was given a thorough makeover by Sir Christopher Wren for the new king, William III, this provides a much more satisfying visit than Buckingham Palace (and it's open year-round). The palace is smaller, and the curators go out of their way to entertain and inform visitors—rather than merely tolerate them, which is the impression you get at Buck House. In 2012 the palace will emerge from its most significant revamp in more than a century, and the palace gardens will be connected to the adjacent Kensington Gardens for the first time since the 19th century. The interior will be reorganized into four "story zones" focusing on the lives of some of its most illustrious former inhabitants, including the monarchs William and Mary, George II, Victoria, and the princesses Margaret and Diana. ⏱ *2 hr. Kensington Gardens. ☎ 0844/482-7777. www.hrp.org.uk/Kensington Palace/. Adults £12.50, £11 seniors, £6.25 children 5–15, free for children 4 & under. Daily Mar–Sept 10am–6pm, Oct–Feb 10am–5pm. Tube: High St. Kensington.*

The gardens at Kensington Palace.

Literary London

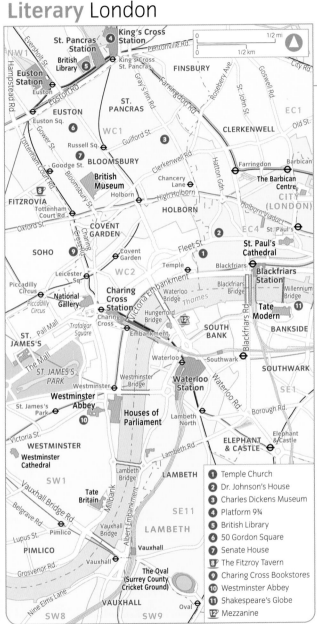

1 Temple Church
2 Dr. Johnson's House
3 Charles Dickens Museum
4 Platform 9¾
5 British Library
6 50 Gordon Square
7 Senate House
8 The Fitzroy Tavern
9 Charing Cross Bookstores
10 Westminster Abbey
11 Shakespeare's Globe
12 Mezzanine

From Shakespeare premiering his plays at the Globe to Dickens illuminating the plight of the backstreet poor, London and literature have long gone together like a good book and a comfy armchair. This tour takes you to sites associated with the city's most illustrious writers, as well as places where you can take a closer look at the works themselves. START: **Tube to Temple.**

1 Temple Church. Its pivotal role in *The Da Vinci Code,* the biggest-selling English language book of the 21st century, has seen this 12th-century church enjoy a significant increase in visitors over the past few years. Built by the Knights Templar, a group of warrior priests who fought in the Crusades, its distinctive circular nave is based on the Church of the Holy Sepulcher in Jerusalem. Within are effigy tombs of various crusaders. ⊕ *30 min. King's Bench Walk.* ☎ *020/7353-3470. www.templechurch.com. Adults £3; free for 20 and under, and seniors. Mon–Tues & Fri 11am–12:30pm & 1–4pm, Wed 2–4pm, Thurs 11am–12:30pm & 2–3:30pm, Sat 11am–12:30pm & 1–3pm, Sun 1–3pm. Tube: Temple.*

2 ★★ Dr. Johnson's House. Travel writers have long been grateful to Dr. Samuel Johnson. His proud maxim, "When a man is tired of

London, he is tired of life…" has kicked off many an introduction to the city. But Johnson was more than a mere quotation machine. One of the great scholars of the 18th century, he was also a poet, a biographer, a critic, and the compiler of one of the first and most influential English-language dictionaries. He worked on his mighty tome over a period of 9 years at this Queen Anne House, which has been restored to its mid-18th century prime and is filled with Johnson-related paraphernalia. ⊕ *30 min. 17 Gough Sq.* ☎ *020/ 7353-3745. wwwdrjohnsonhouse. org. Adults £4.50, £3.50 seniors, £1.50 children. Oct–Apr Mon–Sat 11am–5pm, May–Sept Mon–Sat 11am–5:30pm. Tube: Chancery Lane.*

3 ★★ Charles Dickens Museum. Due to emerge from an expansion and revamp in 2012 to coincide with the bicentennial of Dickens' birth, this museum is

Dr. Johnson's House.

housed in the only London house of the great Victorian novelist still standing. He only lived here from 1837 to 1840, but, this being Dickens, it was more than enough time to churn out several sizeable classics, including *Nicholas Nickleby* and *Oliver Twist*. The rooms have been restored in period style and are adorned with various mementoes from his life, including a number of original manuscripts and his (presumably reinforced) quill pen. ⏱ *1 hr. 48 Doughty St.* ☎ *020/7405-2127. www.dickensmuseum.com. Adults £6, £4.50 seniors, £3 children. Mon–Sat 10am–5pm, Sun 11am–5pm. Tube: Russell Sq.*

④ ★ kids Platform 9¾. All aboard for the Hogwarts Express! J.K. Rowling's famous fictional train departure point, Platform 9¾, has been brought to (sort of) life at King's Cross Station in the form of a sign and a luggage trolley seemingly stuck halfway through a wall, as if magically passing through. Cameras at the ready. ⏱ *10 min. King's Cross Station, Euston Road. Tube: King's Cross.*

⑤ ★★ kids British Library. The ultimate repository of British literature, the B.L. receives a copy of every single book published in the U.K., amounting to some 14 million volumes stored on 400 miles of bookshelves. The library's current home may be less elegant than its predecessor at the British Museum (p 27, ①), but it's much more user-friendly. At the "Treasures of the British Library" exhibition, you can see some of the library's most precious possessions, including Shakespeare's *First Folio*, Jane Austen's writing desk, and Lewis Carroll's diary. ⏱ *1½ hr. 96 Euston Rd.* ☎ *0843/208-1144. www.bl.uk. Free admission. Mon and Wed–Fri 9:30am–6pm, Tues 9:30am–8pm, Sat 9:30am–5pm, Sun 11am–5pm. Tube: Euston or King's Cross.*

⑥ 50 Gordon Square. A blue plaque marks the headquarters of the Bloomsbury Group, a collection of writers, artists, and economists, including Virginia Woolf, E.M. Forster, and John Maynard Keynes, who met here in the early 20th century when Bloomsbury was the unofficial capital of literary London. ⏱ *10 min. Tube: Euston or Euston Sq.*

⑦ Senate House. Exit the southwest corner of Gordon Square and to the south you'll see a sinister-looking, roughly pyramid-shaped building with long, narrow windows. This is Senate House, the basis for the "Ministry of Truth" in George Orwell's *1984*, and where Orwell's wife, Evelyn Waugh, and Dorothy L. Sayers worked during World War II. It's now part of the University of London. ⏱ *5 min. Malet St. Tube: Goodge St.*

British Library.

8 ★★ **The Fitzroy Tavern** was a noted boozy hangout for writers between the 1920s and 1950s, including George Orwell and Dylan Thomas (there's a picture on the wall of Thomas drinking in the pub). Now owned by the Sam Smith's brewery chain, it offers reasonably priced drinks and simple pub food. *16 Charlotte St.* ☎ *020/7580-3714. £.*

9 ★ **Charing Cross Bookstores.** The stretch of Charing Cross Road between Leicester Square and Oxford Street (notwithstanding the current Crossrail diversion) boasts several venerable secondhand and antiquarian bookstores, including Henry Pordes (No. 58), Any Amount of Books (No. 56), and the mighty, multistory Foyles (currently at 113–119, but due to move just down the road in the next couple of years). ⏱ *30 min. Tube: Leicester Sq.*

10 ★★★ **Westminster Abbey.** Poets' Corner in the abbey's south transept is a memorial-smorgasbord of illustrious dead British writers. Chaucer, Dickens, Hardy, Tennyson, and Kipling (among others) are all buried here, while clustered around are memorials to many of the country's other great men (and a few women) of letters, including Milton, Robert Burns, the Brontë sisters, Keats, Jane Austen, D.H. Lawrence and, of course, the big fella himself, Shakespeare. ⏱ *1½ hr. See p 10,* **1**.

11 ★★ **Shakespeare's Globe.** At the on-site exhibition you can find out all about Shakespeare, Shakespeare's London, and the theatres (both past and present) where

Poets' Corner, Westminster Abbey.

his works have been performed. Guided tours are offered daily in the off-season. From May to September, they are available only in the morning. In the afternoon, when matinee performances are taking place, alternative tours to the rather limited remains of the Rose Theatre, the Globe's predecessor, are offered instead. ⏱ *1 hr. See p 12,* **7**.

The Royal National Theatre's **12** ★★ **Mezzanine** restaurant is the ideal place to fortify yourself before a night at the theatre. The menu is European, the setting cheerfully minimal, and the food comes out quickly, to get you seated as soon as possible in front of one of the venue's three stages. *Two courses for £22.50. Royal National Theatre, South Bank.* ☎ *020/7452-3600. ££.*

Kids' London

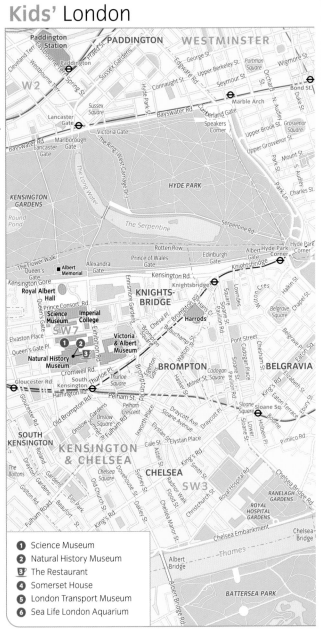

1 Science Museum
2 Natural History Museum
3 The Restaurant
4 Somerset House
5 London Transport Museum
6 Sea Life London Aquarium

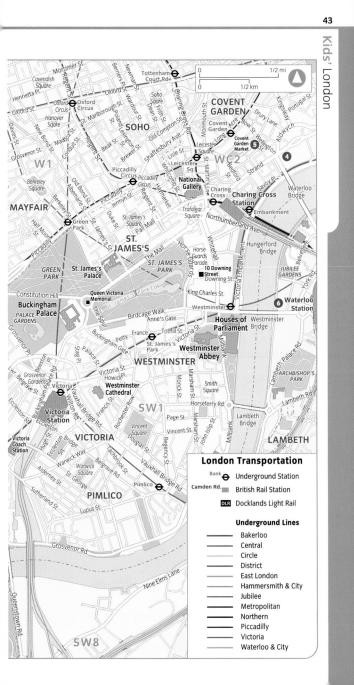

Mortimer St.

Cavendish Square

Henrietta Pl.
Hanover Sqare
Oxford Circus
Oxford Circus
Oxford St.

Regent St.
Newman St.
Berners St.
Wardour St.
Poland St.
Gt. Marlborough St.

Soho Sqare

Tottenham Court Rd.

COVENT GARDEN

Charing Cross Rd.

Kingsway

Portugal St.

Drury Lane

Dean St.
Frith St.
Greek St.

SOHO

Monmouth St.
Bow St.
Long Acre

Covent Garden

Covent Garden Market 5

4

Wellington St.

Aldwych

Davies St.
New Bond St.
Maddox St.
Conduit St.

Lisle St.

WC2

Bedford St.

Strand

Grosvenor St.

W 1

Old Bond St.
Albemarle St.

Beak St.
Brewer St.

Leicester Sqare

St. Martin's Lane

Savoy Pl.

Waterloo Bridge

Berkeley Square

Piccadilly Circus
Piccadilly Circus

Leicester Sq.

National Gallery

Charing Cross

Charing Cross Station

Embankment

Jermyn St.
Regent St.
Haymarket

Trafalgar Square

Northumberland Ave.

MAYFAIR

Green Park

Duke St.

St. James's Square

Pall Mall

The Mall

Whitehall

Hungerford Bridge

Half Moon St.

Piccadilly

St. James's St.

ST. JAMES'S

Horse Guards Rd.

Horse Guards Parade

10 Downing Street
Downing St.

Victoria Embankment

JUBILEE GARDENS

York Rd.

GREEN PARK

St. James's Palace

ST. JAMES'S PARK

King Charles St.

6

Waterloo Station

Constitution Hill

Buckingham Palace

Queen Victoria Memorial

St. James's Park Lake

Birdcage Walk

Anne's Gate

Westminster

Houses of Parliament

Westminster Bridge

PALACE GARDENS

The Spur

Buckingham Gate

Petty France

Tothill St.

St. James's Park

Victoria St.

Millbank

Grosvenor Pl.

Stag Pl.
Palace St.

Westminster Abbey

Grosvenor Gardens
Victoria St.
Howick Pl.

WESTMINSTER

ARCHBISHOP'S PARK

Lwr. Belgrave St.
Buckingham Palace Rd.
Wilton Rd.
Vauxhall Bridge Rd.

Victoria Station

Westminster Cathedral

Francis St.

Monck St.
Marsham St.

Smith Square

Lambeth Palace Rd.
Lambeth Rd.

Eccleston St.

Rochester Row

Horseferry Rd.

SW1

Page St.

Lambeth Bridge

Victoria Coach Station

Hugh St.
Eccleston Sq.

VICTORIA

Belgrave Rd.

Vincent Square
Douglas St.

Vincent St.

John Islip St.
Marsham St.

LAMBETH

Warwick Way

Tachbrook St.

Regency St.

Millbank

Alderney St.
St. George's

Warwick Square

Pimlico

Vauxhall Bridge Rd.

Sutherland St.

PIMLICO

Lupus St.

Grosvenor Rd.

Nine Elms Lane

Queenstown Rd.

SW8

London Transportation

Bank $\oplus$	Underground Station
Camden Rd. ▪	British Rail Station
DLR	Docklands Light Rail

Underground Lines

— Bakerloo
— Central
— Circle
— District
— East London
— Hammersmith & City
— Jubilee
— Metropolitan
— Northern
— Piccadilly
— Victoria
— Waterloo & City

London is one of Europe's best playgrounds for kids. Nearly all the city's major museums have developed well-thought-out activities to entertain and inspire kids on weekends and to show off the collections to their best advantage. Whether you make it to all the venues on this tour obviously depends on the temperaments and ages of your children. START: **Tube to South Kensington.**

1 ★★★ kids Science Museum. Packed with hands-on fun, this great institution appeals to children (and adults) of all ages, with seven levels of exhibits tracing the progress of technology and providing plenty of buttons to press and levers to pull along the way. Dedicated sections for kids include The Garden, an interactive play area for 3- to 6-year-olds on the Lower Ground Floor, and "Launchpad" with more than 50 hands-on experiments. The museum also stages numerous free events for children, including storytelling workshops, and there are daily tours of the galleries. The gift shop is almost as interesting as the exhibits. 🕐 *2 hr. Visit on weekdays to avoid weekend throngs. Exhibition Rd. ☎ 0870/870-4868. www.science museum.org.uk. Free admission, except for special exhibitions. Daily 10am–6pm. Tube: S. Kensington.*

2 ★★★ kids Natural History Museum. This museum's 19th-century building alone is worth a look, with relief statues of beasts incorporated into its terracotta facade. Although not as edgy as the Science Museum next door, this museum is no fossil. Exhibits here include dinosaur displays—a diplod-ocus cast looms down upon you just past the entrance—and there are growling, prowling animatronic beasts—an interactive rainforest, and top-notch mineral and meteor-ite displays. The old animal diora-mas are still around, but the Darwin Wing (a £70-million project) has left them in the dust; its highlights include audiovisual shows and inter-active events with naturalists and photographers (not to mention its 28 million insects and 6 million plant specimens). Free discovery guides, "Explorer" backpacks, and family

Animatronic dinosaurs in the Natural History Museum.

workshops are also available. ⏲ 1½ hr. Cromwell Rd., off Exhibition Rd. ☎ 020/7942-5000. www.nhm.ac.uk. Free admission, except for temporary exhibits. Daily 10am–5:50pm. Tube: S. Kensington.

3 kids **The Restaurant,** set next to the Natural History Museum's Creepy Crawlies exhibit, has a children's "Scoffasaurus" menu, high chairs, and extra space for buggies. The food is basic fare—pizza, burgers, sandwiches, and so on—but decently prepared. *Natural History Museum, Cromwell Rd.* ☎ 020/7942-5000. £.

Sea Life London Aquarium.

4 ★★ kids **Somerset House.** The central courtyard is the real draw at this grand 18th-century riverside building. In summer children can play among 55 water jets that have been programmed to "dance," while in winter they can slide and topple on a temporary ice rink. Free family workshops, usually involving a craft activity, are put on every Saturday afternoon, and if you fancy something a little more highbrow you could pop along to the **Courtauld Gallery,** with its celebrated collection of Impressionist works (tickets are £6 adults, free for children 17 and under, and free for everyone on Mon till 2pm). ⏲ 1 hr. Strand. ☎ 020/7845-4600. www.somersethouse.org.uk. Free admission to courtyard. Daily 10am–6pm. Tube: Temple, Covent Garden, or Charing Cross.

5 ★★★ kids **London Transport Museum.** If only the real London Transport system were as up to date and well maintained as this museum. Tracing the history of the capital's public transport network, the museum gives you the chance to climb aboard a stagecoach, ride a double-decker omnibus, and peer inside an underground train. Family trails are available at the front desk and there's a dedicated hands-on gallery for kids where they can explore miniature buses, trams, trains, and tubes. ⏲ 1½ hr. Covent Garden Piazza. ☎ 020/7379-6344. www.ltmuseum.co.uk. Adults £13.50, £10 seniors, £6.50 students, free for children 15 & under. Sat–Thurs 10am–6pm, Fri 11am–6pm. Tube: Covent Garden.

6 ★★ kids **Sea Life London Aquarium.** You'd expect a bit more for your money at a big-city aquarium but, when it comes down to it, kids adore this place. There's a petting tank of manta rays, a simulated coral reef with sea horses, and plenty of fearsome-looking sharks. ⏲ 1 hr. County Hall, Westminster Bridge Rd. ☎ 020/7967-8000. www.londonaquarium.co.uk. Adults £18, £16.50 seniors, £12.50 children 3–15, free for children 2 & under, £55 family. 10% discount for purchasing tickets online. Mon–Thurs 10am–6pm, Fri–Sun 10am–7pm. Tube: Westminster or Waterloo.

Hampton Court Palace

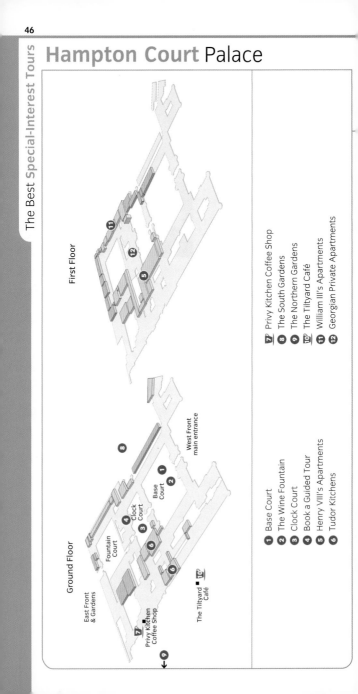

First Floor

Ground Floor

East Front & Gardens

Fountain Court

Clock Court

Base Court

West Front main entrance

Privy Kitchen Coffee Shop

The Tiltyard Café

1 Base Court
2 The Wine Fountain
3 Clock Court
4 Book a Guided Tour
5 Henry VIII's Apartments
6 Tudor Kitchens
7 Privy Kitchen Coffee Shop
8 The South Gardens
9 The Northern Gardens
10 The Tiltyard Café
11 William III's Apartments
12 Georgian Private Apartments

This Tudor masterpiece was built by Cardinal Thomas Wolsey in 1514, only to be snatched up by Henry VIII (1509–47) when Wolsey fell out of favor. It served as a royal residence from 1528 to 1737. Tread the same paths as Elizabeth I, William III, and George II as you learn about life at court through the centuries.

START: **Waterloo railway station for Hampton Court.**

❶ Base Court. Monarchs arrived at Hampton Court via the Thames and entered via the gardens. Visitors today, however, pass through a gatehouse built by Henry VIII for the common folk, and into the Tudor-style courtyard, which is almost exactly as it was when Cardinal Wolsey first built it in 1515. The turrets surrounding the courtyard sport the insignia of Henry VIII and Elizabeth I (who both resided here), as well as numerous carved heads of Roman emperors. 🕐 *10 min.*

❷ ★ The Wine Fountain. The latest addition to this composite palace arrived in 2010 in the form of a replica wine fountain built over the foundations of a Tudor original, discovered 2 years previously on the south side of the Base Court. The design is based on a representation of the *Field of the Cloth of Gold*

painting, which hangs in the Young Henry Exhibition inside the palace. For most of the year the 4-m (13-ft.) high fountain, adorned with 40 gilded lions' heads, pours water from its eight taps, but has been adapted to occasionally serve something a little stronger—just as in Henry's day. 🕐 *10 min.*

❸ ★★ Clock Court. From the Base Court, pass through the Anne Boleyn Gatehouse (built in the 19th century, long after the beheaded queen's death) and into the Clock Court, which encompasses several architectural styles, ranging from Tudor (the north side) to 18th-century Gothic (the east side). The major attraction is the elaborate Astronomical Clock, built for Henry VIII (note the sun revolving around the Earth—the clock was built before Galileo and Copernicus debunked that myth). 🕐 *15 min.*

Hampton Court Palace.

How to Get to Hampton Court

Hampton Court Palace is located in East Molesey, Surrey, 13 miles west of London. Trains from London's Waterloo Station to Hampton Court Station take 35 minutes; when you exit the station, turn right and follow the signs to the palace, a 10-minute walk away. Alternatively, Westminster Passenger Service Association (☎ 020/7930-2062; www.wpsa.co.uk; Tube: Westminster) operates a riverboat service from Westminster Pier to Hampton Court. Boats leave daily at 10:30am, 11:15am, and noon. Journey time varies between half an hour and four hours, depending on the conditions. Round-trip tickets cost £22.50 for adults, £15 for seniors, £11.25 for children aged 4 to 14, and £56.25 for a family ticket; one child aged 3 or younger accompanied by an adult goes free.

④ ★★★ kids Book a Guided Tour. Stop in at the Information Centre inside the baroque colonnade on the south side of the Clock Court and book a spot on one of the day's costumed guided tours (included with your admission fee). The guides here are knowledgeable and entertaining, and dispense juicy historical tidbits. Kids especially enjoy the experience. You must book in person; do so as soon as you get to the palace, as space on these tours is limited. If you have a choice, opt for the tour of the Henry VIII State Apartments or the King's Apartments. Self-guided palace audio tours are also available (and free). ⏱ *10 min.*

⑤ ★★★ Henry VIII's Apartments. Even though Sir Christopher Wren modified some of them, these rooms represent the best examples of Tudor style in England. Don't miss the elaborately gilded ceiling of the **Chapel Royal,** a still-functioning church where Henry was informed of the "misconduct" of his adulterous fifth wife, Catherine Howard, and later married wife number six, Catherine Parr. Right off the chapel is the **Haunted Gallery,** where Howard's ghost reportedly still pleads for her life. The **Watching Chamber,** where senior courtiers would dine, is the only one of Henry VIII's many English estate rooms in something close to its original form (the fireplace and stained glass are not originals). Also impressive is the **Great Hall,** with a set of tapestries (real gold and silver thread) that cost Henry as much as his naval fleet. ⏱ *45 min.*

⑥ ★★ Tudor Kitchens. At its peak, Hampton Court's kitchen staff catered two meals a day to a household of 600—more than any modern hotel. An enormous effort of labor prepared and served up some 8,200 sheep, 1,240 oxen, and 600,000 gallons of beer a year. Once the palace lost its popularity with the royal set, the 50-room kitchens were converted into apartments. They were restored in 1991 and today live Tudor cookery demonstrations are put on throughout the year. Check the website for dates. ⏱ *45 min.*

The atmospheric **7 ★ kids Privy Kitchen Coffee Shop** offers a Tudor-style atmosphere (think wooden tables and 16th-century-style chandeliers) along with decent pastries, light lunches, and afternoon tea. £.

8 ★★★ The South Gardens. The palace's southern gardens are home to William III's **Privy Garden,** with its elaborate baroque ironwork screen; the box-hedged **Knot Garden,** which resembles a traditional Tudor garden; and the lovely sunken **Pond Gardens.** The **Great Vine** is one of the oldest (planted in 1768) and largest grape vines in the world. The annual 270kg (600 lb) crop is sold to the public after the August Bank Holiday. If the weather is poor, head to the Orangery for Mantegna's nine-painting masterpiece, *Triumph of Caesar,* one of the most important works of the Italian Renaissance. 🕐 **40 min.**

9 ★★ kids The Northern Gardens. Renowned for their spring bulbs, the Northern Gardens are where you'll find the palace's

The palace's famous Hedge Maze.

famous **Hedge Maze,** whose labyrinthine paths cover nearly a half-mile. Planted in 1702, the maze has trapped many a visitor in its clutches. When you do escape, stroll to the adjacent **Tiltyard** (jousting area), where you'll find several smaller gardens, as well as the only surviving tiltyard tower (used to seat spectators at tournaments) built by Henry VIII. 🕐 **30–45 min.**

The sunken Pond Gardens.

10 ★ **The Tiltyard Café** offers well-priced sandwiches, salads, afternoon teas, and light meals in a slightly upscale setting. If the weather is good, try to sit on the outdoor terrace. You can also picnic on the grass around the cafe, or on the benches in the Clock Court. £.

11 ★★★ **William III's Apartments.** These baroque rooms (among the finest of their kind) were designed by Sir Christopher Wren for William III (r. 1689–1702), who did more to shape the palace than any other monarch, though he died shortly after moving in. The apartments were badly damaged in a 1986 fire (you can still see scorch marks on the ceiling in the **Privy Chamber**) but have been fully restored. All the rooms in this wing are impressive, but the **Guard Chamber** features a spectacular collection of nearly 3,000 weapons; the **Presence Chamber** has an exquisite rock-crystal chandelier; the **Private Dining Room** has a

reproduction of the king's gold-plated dining service and the **Great Bedchamber** (ceremonial only—the king slept elsewhere) is loaded with gilded furniture, priceless tapestries, and a magnificent red-velvet canopy bed. 🕐 *1 hr.*

12 ★★ **Georgian Private Apartments.** The private apartments of George II and Queen Caroline still look as they did in 1737, when Caroline died and the royal court left the palace behind forever. The **Presence Chamber** of the 10-year-old Duke of Cumberland (the king's second son) is the only room at the palace that's fully paneled, gilded, and painted. Only a portion of the ceiling of the **Wolsey Closet** is from the Tudor era, though the ceiling is decorated in the Renaissance style. The state bed in the **Queen's Bedchamber** is a reproduction. If the king and queen wanted to sleep together in privacy (which was no mean feat for the royal couple), it was to this room they retired, thanks to a rather sophisticated door lock. 🕐 *45 min.* ●

Practical Matters—Hampton Court

Admission to the palace and gardens costs £15.95 adults, £8 children 5 to 16, £13.20 seniors and students, £43.46 family (2 adults, 3 children). To avoid waiting in line, and to obtain around a 10% discount per ticket, book your tickets on the website (☎ 0844/482-7777; www.hrp.org.uk) (tickets are valid for 1 week from the time of purchase). The admission fee also includes a guided tour and/or a self-guided audio tour; inquire at the Information Center inside the Clock Court (**3**).

The palace is open daily from 10am to 6pm from April to October (the best time to visit), daily 10am to 4:30pm from November to March. The gardens are open 7am until dusk. Closed December 24, 25, and 26. Arrive at opening time to beat the crowds.

Chelsea

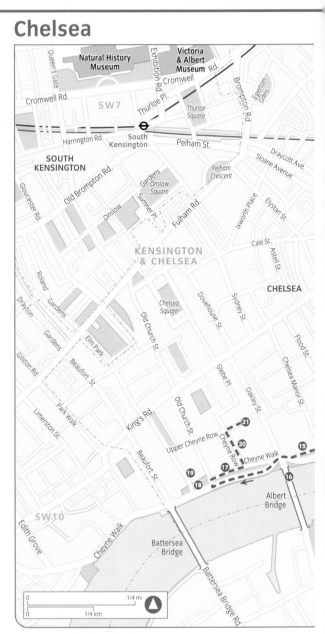

Previous page: Columbia Road Market.

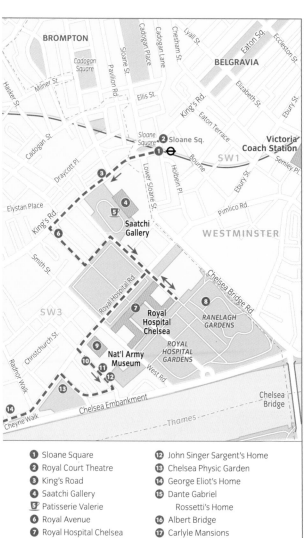

1. Sloane Square
2. Royal Court Theatre
3. King's Road
4. Saatchi Gallery
5. Patisserie Valerie
6. Royal Avenue
7. Royal Hospital Chelsea
8. Ranelagh Gardens
9. National Army Museum
10. Oscar Wilde's Home
11. Augustus John's Studio
12. John Singer Sargent's Home
13. Chelsea Physic Garden
14. George Eliot's Home
15. Dante Gabriel
    Rossetti's Home
16. Albert Bridge
17. Carlyle Mansions
18. Statue of Sir Thomas More
19. Chelsea Old Church
20. Thomas Carlyle's House
21. Leigh Hunt's Home

Since the 16th century, when Henry VIII and Thomas More built country manors on its riverbanks, Chelsea has had a long tradition of eccentricity, aristocracy, and artisanship. This posh district is great for a stroll. Keep an eye peeled for blue plaques affixed to houses; they reveal the many leading figures who once called this neighborhood home. START: **Tube to Sloane Square.**

1 Sloane Square. Royal physician Sir Hans Sloane (1660–1753), who helped found the British Museum, is the namesake of this busy square, marking the boundary between the well-to-do districts of Chelsea and Belgravia. In addition to his educational and medical achievements, Sloane discovered the milk chocolate recipe that became the basis of the Cadbury chocolate empire. *Intersection of Sloane St. & King's Rd.*

2 ★★ Royal Court Theatre. This restored theatre, originally built in 1888, is famous for showcasing playwrights such as George Bernard Shaw, John Osborne, and Harold Pinter. Nowadays, the work of today's most promising dramatists is performed on the two stages. *A few steps to the right of the Sloane Sq. Tube exit.* ☎ 020/7565 5000. www.royalcourttheatre.com.

3 ★★ King's Road. Chelsea's main road was once an exclusive royal passage used by Charles II to go from Whitehall to Hampton Court. It was also a favorite route of highwaymen looking to "liberate" royal goods. An echo of these King's Road robbers can be found in the extortionate prices of its chichi stores that once helped the 1960s' swing and '70s punks look the part, and today attracts free-spending members of London's upper social strata. *Runs from Sloane Sq. southwest to Putney Bridge.*

4 ★★★ Saatchi Gallery. The capital's largest contemporary art gallery stands just off the King's Road. The brainchild of ad mogul and mega-collector Charles Saatchi, it lays on a succession of temporary exhibitions dedicated to all that is best, brightest, and most challenging in the modern art world.

Saatchi Gallery.

Royal Hospital Chelsea.

Whatever's on display when you visit, it's liable to be controversial—or the gallery isn't really doing its job. *Duke of York's Headquarters, King's Road.* ☎ *020/7811-30370. www.saatchi-gallery.co.uk. Free admission. Daily 10am–6pm.*

Duke of York Square has a number of good dining spots, but you can't go wrong at this branch of **5** ★ **Patisserie Valerie.** Hot dishes, salads, and sandwiches are reliably good; and the desserts are killer. Try the oversize croissants for breakfast. *81 Duke of York Sq. (off King's Rd.). 020/7730-7094. £.*

6 ★ **Royal Avenue.** This small, picturesque road was not quite what William III intended in the 1690s. He wanted it to run all the way from the nearby Chelsea Royal Hospital to Kensington Palace, but construction was cut short after his death. Still, it proved just the ticket for its most famous fictional resident, Ian Fleming's James Bond. *Between St. Leonard's Terrace & King's Rd.*

7 ★★ **Royal Hospital Chelsea.** This Christopher Wren masterpiece, commissioned by Charles II in 1692 as a retirement estate for injured and old soldiers, is still home to 400-plus "Chelsea Pensioners," who dress in traditional red uniforms and offer informative tours of the historic grounds and chapel. There's also a small on-site museum and the grounds host the prestigious Chelsea Flower Show, held every May since 1912. *Royal Hospital Rd.* ☎ *020/7881-5200. www.chelsea-pensioners.co.uk. Free admission. Guided tours by prior arrangement only. Mon–Sat 10am–noon, 2–4pm, Sun 2–4pm. Church services open to public, Sun 10:30am.*

8 ★ **Ranelagh Gardens.** Once centered round a large rotunda (demolished in 1805), these gardens (some of the prettiest in London) were a favorite of 18th-century socialites who were occasionally entertained here by a young Mozart. *At Chelsea Royal Hospital. Free admission. Mon–Sat 10am–noon, 2–4pm, Sun 2–4pm.*

9 ★★ **National Army Museum.** Home to the Duke of Wellington's shaving mirror and Florence Nightingale's lamp, plus plenty of assorted weapons, this museum follows the history of Britain's fighting forces from 1066 to the present. *Royal Hospital Rd.* ☎ *020/7730-0717. www.nam.ac.uk. Free admission. Daily 10am–5:30pm.*

10 ★ **Oscar Wilde's Home.** The eccentricities of Oscar and his wife Constance (they lived here from 1885–95) were well known to neighbors, who would often see them on the street dressed in velvet (him) and a huge Gainsborough hat (her). Street boys would shout, "'Ere comes 'Amlet and Ophelia!" The house is not open to the public, but is marked with a blue plaque. *34 Tite St.*

⓫ Augustus John's Studio. A renowned Welsh painter (1878–1961), John was one of Chelsea's most illustrious artists. His insightful portraits and landscapes made him famous, while his bohemian lifestyle and love affairs (including one with the mother of James Bond creator, Ian Fleming) earned him notoriety. *33 Tite St.*

⓬ ★ John Singer Sargent's Home. The renowned American portraitist of the high and mighty lived and worked at this address (the former abode of the equally famous artist James McNeill Whistler) from 1901 until his death in 1925. *31 Tite St.*

⓭ ★★ Chelsea Physic Garden. This garden was established in 1673 by the Apothecaries' Company to cultivate medicinal plants and herbs. Cotton seeds from the garden were sent to America in 1732, and slavery became their eventual harvest. *66 Royal Hospital Rd.* ☎ *020/7352-5646. www.chelseaphysicgarden. co.uk. Adults £8, £5 children 5–15. Apr–Oct Tues–Fri noon–5pm, Sun noon–6pm.*

⓮ George Eliot's Home. The famous Victorian novelist, born Mary Ann Evans in 1819, moved into this house with her new and much younger husband, John Cross, only a few months before her death in December 1880. *4 Cheyne Walk.*

⓯ Dante Gabriel Rossetti's Home. The eccentric pre-Raphaelite poet and painter (1828–82) lived here after the death of his wife in 1862. He kept a menagerie of exotic animals, including kangaroos, a white bull, peacocks, and a wombat that inspired his friend, Lewis Carroll, to create the Dormouse in *Alice in Wonderland*. *16 Cheyne Walk.*

⓰ ★★ Albert Bridge. Designed by R. M. Ordish, this picturesque suspension bridge linking Battersea and Chelsea was completed in 1873. Conservationists kept the bridge from destruction in the 1950s. In 1973, the cast-iron structure had new supports installed so it could cope with the rigors of modern traffic, though it still tends to shake when things get busy (hence its

Chelsea Physic Garden.

nickname, the "Trembling Lady"). At night it's illuminated by 4,000 bulbs.

17 Carlyle Mansions. Henry James (1843–1916), the great American novelist *(Portrait of a Lady)*, was sick in bed inside this riverside flat when he was honored for his work (and for taking British citizenship) with the Order of the British Empire. Only a few weeks later, the writer drew his last breath here. *Cheyne Walk.*

18 ★ Statue of Sir Thomas More. Despite his long friendship with Henry VIII, Lord Chancellor Thomas More (1478–1535) refused to accept Henry as head of the Church of England after the king's notorious break with the Roman Catholic Church. More paid for his religious convictions with his life— he was tried and subsequently beheaded for treason. In 1935, the Roman Catholic Church canonized him as the patron saint of lawyers and politicians. *Old Church St.*

19 ★ Chelsea Old Church. A church has stood on this site since 1157. Though the structure suffered serious damage during the Blitz, it has since been rebuilt and restored. Sir Thomas More worshiped here (he built the South Chapel in 1528), and it was the setting for Henry VIII's secret marriage to third wife Jane Seymour in 1536. *64 Cheyne Walk.* ☎ 020/7795-1019. www.chelsea oldchurch.org.uk. Free admission. Tues, Wed & Thurs 2–4pm.

Statue of Sir Thomas More.

20 ★★ Thomas Carlyle's House. The famous Scottish historian (1795–1881) and his wife, Jane, entertained their friends Dickens and Chopin here. It was in this remarkably well-preserved Victorian home that the "Sage of Chelsea" finished his important *History of the French Revolution. 24 Cheyne Row.* ☎ 020/7352-7087. www.national trust.org.uk/main/w-carlyleshouse. Adults £5.10, £2.60 children 5–16. Mar–Oct Wed–Sun 11am–5pm.

21 Leigh Hunt's Home. From 1833 to 1840, the noted poet and essayist (a friend of Byron and Keats) lived here, and was well known for pestering neighbors for loans. His wife infuriated Jane Carlyle, the celebrated Victorian letter writer and wife of the historian Thomas, by incessantly borrowing household items. *22 Upper Cheyne Row.*

Plaque outside Thomas Carlyle's House.

Mayfair

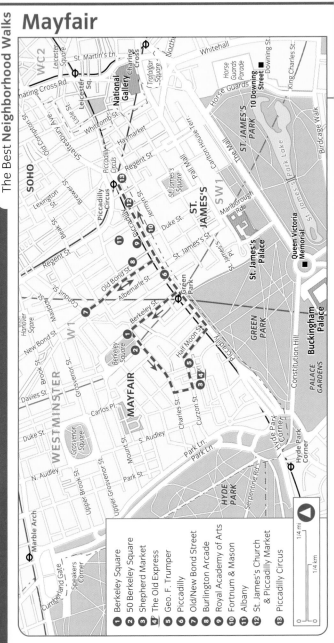

For more than 3 centuries, Mayfair has been an exclusive neighborhood of the aristocracy, who used to live in grand style inside elegant mansions run by armies of servants. Enough of these urban palaces survive to make a walk through Mayfair a fascinating glimpse into how London's rich lived—and still live. This walk focuses on the southern part of Mayfair. START: **Green Park Tube Station.**

1 ★ Berkeley Square. Laid out in the 18th century on part of Lord Berkeley's London estate, this grand square has long been one of the capital's most-sought-after addresses. Notables who have called the square home include prime ministers Winston Churchill (who lived at No. 48 as a boy) and George Canning (who resided briefly at No. 50; see **2**). Among the lovely old houses on the west side is Lansdowne House, on the southwest corner, designed by famed Scottish architect Robert Adam; the modern east side is now undistinguished office buildings. The plane trees surrounding the square were planted in 1789 and are among the oldest in the city.

2 50 Berkeley Square. This Georgian-style building (now home to a rare-books shop) was known as the "most haunted house in London" in the 19th century, when sightings of a bewigged man and sounds of an unearthly nature kept the house untenanted. Although strange happenings have been reported here in recent years, the worst of it seems

to have taken place in Victorian days, when an evil presence so terrified a visitor that he threw himself out the window and was impaled on the railings below.

3 ★★ Shepherd Market. In the mid-18th century, the riotous May Fair (the neighborhood's namesake) was banned and the land redeveloped by architect Edward Shepherd. The result was much what you see now: Charming yet humble buildings from the days when this area was the hub of the servant classes in Mayfair. Today it's filled with great traditional pubs, including the 1730s'-built Shepherd Tavern, and restaurants serving various different cuisines—French, Italian, Lebanese, Mexican, Polish, and more.

A favorite with the locals, **4 ★★ The Old Express** serves great old English staples, such as fish and chips, sausages and mash, and cottage pie. *30 Shepherd Market.* ☎ *020/7499-1299. www.theold express.co.uk. ££.*

The leafy Berkeley Square.

The upmarket Burlington Arcade.

⑤ ★ **Geo. F. Trumper.** This English institution opened in 1875, and still offers traditional wet shaves with straight razors and hot towels, mustache trimming, and—in a concession to metrosexual modernity—manicures. Even if you don't need a shave or toiletries, do have a look around this wonderful shop. *9 Curzon St.* ☎ *020/7499-1850. www.trumpers.com.*

⑥ ★★ **Piccadilly.** The name Piccadilly is said to have come from the word "picadil," a stiff collar manufactured by an early-17th-century tailor who bought a great parcel of land here on which he built a grand

home. Lest the upstart forget his humble beginnings, it was sneeringly referred to as "Piccadilly Hall." In the 18th and 19th centuries, many great mansions were built along the street facing Green Park. Head east on Piccadilly so you can admire the elaborate gates surrounding Green Park and the carved classical-style heads on the Parisian-inspired facade of the **Ritz** hotel.

⑦ ★★★ **Old/New Bond Street.** Perhaps the smartest shopping street in London, lined from end to end by boutiques from some of the biggest names in fashion and jewelry (such as Nicole Farhi, Louis Vuitton, and Bulgari), and not a price tag in sight (if you have to ask…). The point where Old Bond Street meets New is marked with a statue showing President Roosevelt and prime minister Churchill chatting on a bench.

⑧ ★★ **Burlington Arcade.** Opened in the early 19th century, this is a very superior shopping center, with around 40 elegant shops (with curved glass windows and mahogany fronts) selling upmarket clothing, shoes, art, and antiques. Top-hatted, frock-coated guards are employed to make sure nobody does anything as uncouth as to run, whistle, or sing.

The spiral staircase at Fortnum & Mason.

61

Mayfair

9 ★★★ Royal Academy of Arts.
Burlington House, built in the 1660s, was a magnificent estate purchased by the government in 1854 to house England's oldest arts society. The Royal Academy has staged a "Summer Exhibition" for more than 200 years now, along with popular temporary exhibitions. Free tours of the permanent collection are given at 1pm Tuesday, 1 and 4pm Wednesday to Friday, and 11:30am Saturday. *Burlington House, Piccadilly.* ☎ *020/7300-8000. www.royalacademy.org.uk. Sat–Thurs 10am–6pm, Fri 10am–10pm. Adults £10, seniors £8, children 8–18 £3, free for children 7 & under.*

10 ★★ Fortnum & Mason.
A famous partnership began in 1705 when shop owner Hugh Mason let a room to William Fortnum, a footman for Queen Anne at the Palace of St. James's. The enterprising Fortnum "recycled" candle ends from the palace (the Queen required fresh candles nightly) and sold them to Mason. From this humble beginning, Fortnum & Mason grew to rule Britannia (or at least Piccadilly) with one of the earliest globally recognized brand names. For a refined (if pricey) afternoon tea, try the St. James Restaurant on the fourth floor. See also p 82. *181 Piccadilly.*

11 Albany.
Built in the 1770s by architect William Chambers for Lord Melbourne, this grand Georgian building was turned into a residence for gentlemen in 1802. Since then, many poets (Lord Byron), authors (Graham Greene), and playwrights have all called this prime Piccadilly patch home. *At Albany Court off Piccadilly.*

12 ★★ St. James's Church & Piccadilly Market.
This unprepossessing redbrick church is one of Christopher Wren's simplest, said by

Piccadilly Circus at night.

Charles Dickens to be "not one of the master's happiest efforts." The poet William Blake was baptized here, as was William Pitt, the first earl of Chatham, who became England's youngest prime minister at the age of 24. You are welcome to enter and sit in its quiet interior, or enjoy the free (donations desperately needed) lunchtime recitals. There's a market in the forecourt Tuesday through Saturday, selling crafts, clothes, and collectibles. *197 Piccadilly.* ☎ *020/7734-4511. www.st-james-piccadilly.org.*

13 ★ Piccadilly Circus.
London's slightly underwhelming answer to New York's Times Square was the first place in the city to sport electrical signage, and its glaring neon billboards have graced a million postcards. The word "circus" refers to a circular juncture at an intersection of streets, and the plaza was built in 1819 to connect two of London's major shopping streets: Regent Street and Piccadilly. The statue popularly known as Eros (though, trivia fans note, it's actually Anteros, the Greek god of requited love) on the central island is a favorite meeting place.

Hampstead

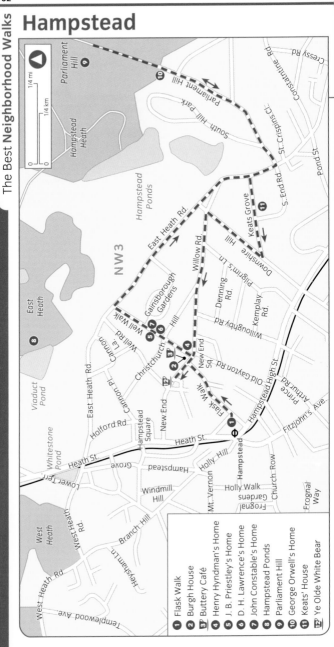

NW3

Parliament Hill

Hampstead Heath

Hampstead Ponds

East Heath

Viaduct Pond

Whitestone Pond

West Heath

1 Flask Walk
2 Burgh House
3 Buttery Café
4 Henry Hyndman's Home
5 J. B. Priestley's Home
6 D. H. Lawrence's Home
7 John Constable's Home
8 Hampstead Ponds
9 Parliament Hill
10 George Orwell's Home
11 Keats' House
12 Ye Olde White Bear

Hampstead first became popular during the Great Plague of 1665, when well-to-do Londoners escaped here from the contagion of their neighborhoods. Today, it is still a charming refuge, known for its historic buildings, rich artistic and literary legacy, and proximity to the Heath, 324 hectares (800 acres) of controlled wilderness and far-reaching views. START: **Tube to Hampstead.**

1 ★ **Flask Walk.** Now a narrow alley of chichi shops leading to a street of expensive homes, Flask Walk was the site of early-18th-century fairs and also home to year-round establishments for drinking and gambling—all built to entertain the crush of Londoners escaping the fetid city streets for Hampstead's fresh air. The street was named after a now-defunct tavern that bottled the village's pure water and sold it throughout London.

2 ★★ **Burgh House.** Built in 1704, this restored Queen Anne structure, the former home of spa physician Dr. William Gibbon, now houses a museum specializing in Hampstead's history. It offers literary-themed walks through the town (and across the common) and puts on classical concerts. *New End Sq.* ☎ *020/7431-0144. www.burgh house.org.uk. Free admission. Wed–Sun noon–5pm.*

Found in the Burgh House basement, the **3** ★★ **Buttery Café** serves great home-made cakes and afternoon tea from 3pm, as well as some heartier traditional British and European dishes. The garden is a great place for a slow lunch on a sunny afternoon. *New End Sq.* ☎ *020/7794-2905. MC, V. ££.*

4 ★ **Henry Hyndman's Home.** A journalist, politician, and public speaker, Hyndman (1842–1921) founded the Social Democratic Federation, England's first socialist

Flask Walk, Hampstead.

party, in 1881. He lived in this house until his death in 1921. *13 Well Walk.*

5 **J. B. Priestley's Home.** One of England's most prolific men of letters, Priestley (1894–1984) was an essayist, playwright, biographer, historian, and social commentator who refused a knighthood and peerage. He lived in this Queen Anne–style house from 1929 to 1931. *27 Well Walk.*

6 **D. H. Lawrence's Home.** During World War I, Lawrence (1885–1930) made his home here after being kicked out of Cornwall when his wife was unjustly accused of being a German spy. He left in 1919 for Italy, where he wrote his most famous novel, *Lady*

Chatterley's Lover, in 1928. The book was banned in Britain on charges of indecency and wasn't published here uncensored until 1960. *32 Well Walk.*

7 John Constable's Home.

The well-known British landscape painter and portraitist resided here from 1827 until his death in 1837. It was in his many studies of nearby Hampstead Heath that Constable mastered the depiction of weather in landscapes, tirelessly painting the same scene under different climatic conditions. The house is marked with a blue plaque. *40 Well Walk.*

8 ★★ Hampstead Ponds.

Hampstead boasts three lovely wooded ponds (actually former reservoirs dug in the mid-19th century) where you can take a refreshing dip. There's a men's pond, a ladies' pond, and a mixed pond, which gets particularly busy in summer. *Hampstead Heath.* ☎ 020/7485-3873. *www.cityoflondon.gov.uk. Admission £2 to the ponds all year, £2 to the lido early morning, evening, and winter, £5 on summer days. Daily mid-Mar–mid-Feb (usually 7am–dusk, but times vary; call ahead).*

9 ★★★ Parliament Hill.

According to legend, the men behind the 1605 Gunpowder Plot planned to watch parliament blown sky-high from this elevated vantage point. Fittingly, it's now one of the best places to watch the fireworks staged every November 5 to commemorate the foiling of the plot. The daytime views are no less dramatic; a map on the site identifies the buildings in the distance. *Inside Hampstead Heath.*

10 ★ George Orwell's Home.

The author of *Animal Farm, 1984,* and *Down and Out in Paris and London,* wrote the satirical *Keep the Aspidistra Flying* in a backroom on an upper floor of this house. He lived here for only 6 months in 1936 while working part-time at Booklover's Corner, a small bookstore on South End Green (it's now a pizzeria). *77 Parliament Hill St.*

The Loos of London

London once had plenty of public lavatories. Time was when nearly every high street boasted its own well-maintained public convenience, but they're now few and far between. The old-fashioned tiled underground facilities have almost completely disappeared (they're too expensive for councils to maintain) while the free-standing kiosks (known locally as "super loos") are increasingly thin on the ground. If you get caught short, however, many of the capital's major train and tube stops have public lavatories, typically costing around 30p. Other options include museums, galleries, and art centers, most of which are free, and offer good-standard facilities, or public parks. Department stores are another good bet, or fast-food restaurants. Come the evening, however, your best option may be to nip into the nearest pub, though you should probably buy a little something to become a customer first.

Swimmers in the mixed pond at Hampstead.

11 ★★ **Keats' House.** Keats lived just 2 years at this Regency house, but found enough time to write some of his most famous works, including *Ode to a Nightingale,* and fall in love with next-door neighbor Fanny Brawne, his eventual fiancée (and the muse behind many of his best works). In 1820, he traveled to Italy, where he died of tuberculosis only a few months later. The house is now a museum dedicated to the poet's life and displays original manuscripts and portraits. Download an audio tour from the website. ⏱ *1hr. Keats Grove.* ☎ *020/7435-2062. www.keatshouse.cityoflondon.gov. uk. Adult £5; children 16 & under free. Apr–Oct Tues–Sun (& Bank Hol Mon) 1–5pm Nov–Mar Fri–Sun 1–5pm.Wed–Sun noon–5pm.*

With dark woodcarvings, fine furniture, and photos of the area's celebs on the walls, **12** ★★**Ye Olde White Bear** manages to project the atmosphere of a country village pub,

even though it's more of a restaurant these days. The great selection of meats and cheeses are all sourced locally. *Corner of Well Rd. and New End Rd.* ☎ *020/7435-3758. £.*

Keats' House.

The City & East End

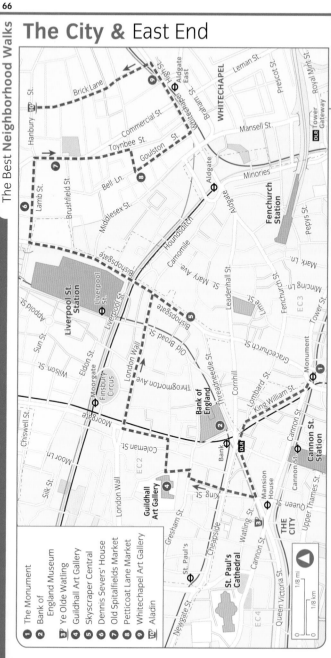

1. The Monument
2. Bank of England Museum
3. Ye Olde Watling
4. Guildhall Art Gallery
5. Skyscraper Central
6. Dennis Severs' House
7. Old Spitalfields Market
8. Petticoat Lane Market
9. Whitechapel Art Gallery
10. Aladin

WHITECHAPEL

THE CITY

St. Paul's Cathedral

This walk starts where it all began in the Square Mile, also known as "the City." The site of the first London settlement founded by the Romans 2,000 years ago continues to thrive as the center of the country's financial services. Onward from here is the East End, where many exciting developments in the arts, shopping, and entertainment take place. START: **Monument Tube Station.**

1 ★★★ kids **The Monument.** Sir Christopher Wren designed this 62m-high (203-ft.) Doric stone column—topped with a gilded fiery urn—to commemorate the Great Fire of 1666. That tragic disaster started on September 2 inside the house of a baker on Pudding Lane (the height of the tower corresponds to the distance from its base to the fire's starting point). A stiff wind ignited the old timber and thatch houses of the City; more than 13,000 houses and 87 churches were reduced to smoldering ashes. It's 311 steps to the top, from where the views are among the finest in the City. ⏱ *50 min. Monument St. ☎ 020/7626-2717. www.the monument.info. Adults £3, £2 seniors, £1 children. Daily 9:30am–5:30pm. Tube: Monument.*

2 ★★ kids **Bank of England Museum.** Take a close-up look at the glue that holds the Square Mile together: money. Exhibits include plenty of old notes and coins, and a recreation of an 18th-century banking hall. The highlight is a genuine gold bar that can be touched but—no matter how you wiggle your hand inside the Perspex box—not removed. ⏱ *45 min. Threadneedle St. ☎ 020/7601-5545. www. bankofengland.co.uk/education/ museum. Free admission. Mon–Fri 10am–5pm. Tube: Bank.*

Just south of St. Mary-le-Bow, the "Cockney Church," is London's oldest road, Watling Street, which 1,900 years ago linked the capital with the coast. Here you'll find the aged—if not quite so venerable— **3** ★ **Ye Olde Watling.** Built in the 17th century out of ships' timbers, it serves some decent pub grub and a range of ales. *29 Watling St. ☎ 020/7248-8935. www.nicholsonspubs.co.uk. £.*

The Monument.

4 ★★ kids **Guildhall Art Gallery.** The modern extension of the City's medieval and much-restored Guildhall holds an art gallery showcasing a rotating selection from its 4,000 plus London-related works. The building also contains a small museum of historic clocks and, in the basement, the remains of London's Roman amphitheatre. ⏲ *1 hr. Guildhall Yard, off Gresham St.* ☎ *020/7332-3700. www.guildhall-art-gallery.org.uk. Adults £2.50, £1 seniors & students, free for children 15 & under. Free Fri and after 3:30pm on all other days. Mon–Sat 10am–5pm, Sun noon–4pm. Tube: Bank.*

5 kids **Skyscraper Central.** Just off Bishopsgate, the small square of Great St. Helen's neatly encapsulates how the City's skyline has changed over the centuries. At its center is the small, almost fragile-looking, 13th-century **St. Helen's church,** while on three sides stand giant modern skyscrapers. From the church courtyard, you can see to the west Tower 42, formerly the City's tallest building (check out the views from the top at the Vertigo 42 champagne bar; see p 121), to the

east the **Gherkin** (more formally known as 30 St. Mary Axe), and to the north, the **Heron Building,** which at 230m (755 ft.) is currently the tallest building in the Square Mile. ⏲ *5 min. Gt. St. Helen's. Tube: Bank.*

6 ★★ **Dennis Severs' House.** From 1979 until his death in 1999, the American expat Dennis Severs not only restored this Spitalfields town house to its early-18th-century prime but also created a fictional back story for it, as a refuge for the Jervises, a family of Huguenots who had fled persecution in France. The rooms have been arranged as if just vacated by their occupants. The result is fascinatingly odd. Note the limited opening hours. ⏲ *1 hr. 18 Folgate St.* ☎ *020/7247-4013. www. dennissevershouse.co.uk. Adults £8 Sun, £12 Mon "Silent Night", £5 Mon lunchtime. Sun noon–4pm, Mon 6–9pm & 1st & 3rd Mon noon–2pm. Tube: Liverpool St.*

7 ★ **Old Spitalfields Market.** Although now surrounded by a modern, upmarket development of high-end shops, restaurants, and delis, the craft market is still holding strong, with stalls selling clothes,

The Gherkin.

Market Sundays

Sundays are a browser's paradise in the East End. Though several markets stay open in low-key fashion throughout the week, on a Sunday morning Spitalfields will be in full swing, while Petticoat Lane will have spilled beyond its usual Wentworth Street parameters, filling the surrounding roads with cheap clothes and jewelry. Just to the east is Brick Lane, which lies at the heart of the Bangladeshi community, and on Sunday the northern end is given over to a hugely vibrant flea market selling everything from furniture and clothes to DVDs. This is complemented by Upmarket, held in the Old Truman Brewery and a sign of the area's recent gentrification. You'll find around 140 stalls selling arts and crafts, vintage clothes, and fashions and, if you fancy stretching your legs, a 5-minute walk north of Brick Lane takes you to Columbia Road and its famous flower market, its stalls piled high with colorful blooms.

secondhand books and records, home-made jewelry, hats, and an assortment of esoteric arts and crafts. At the northern end is a row of cheap Caribbean and Indian food stalls. There's been a market on this site for more than 350 years. ⏱ *45 min. Commercial St.* ☎ *020/7247-8556. Mon–Fri 10am–4pm, Sat 9am–5pm. Tube: Liverpool St.*

8 ★★ **Petticoat Lane Market.** This ever-popular market selling cheap clothes, leather goods, and jewelry was founded more than 400 years ago by Huguenots from France who sold lace items, including the eponymous undergarments. The name was changed to Wentworth Street in the 19th century so as to avoid offending delicate Victorian sensibilities but market traders have long memories, and London's premier cheap clothes market continues to be known by its somewhat racier moniker. ⏱ *45 min. Wentworth St. & Middlesex St.* ☎ *020/7364-1717.*

Mon–Fri 8am–4pm, Sat 9am–2pm. Tube: Liverpool St. or Aldgate East.

9 ★★★ **Whitechapel Art Gallery.** The gallery has been the East End's artistic touchstone for more than a century. Always as close to the cutting edge as possible, it offers constantly changing exhibitions of the best and most challenging contemporary visual art, as well as a program of talks, film screenings, and concerts. ⏱ *1½ hr. 77–82 Whitechapel Rd.* ☎ *020/7522-7888. www.whitechapelgallery.org. Free admission. Tues–Sun 11am–6pm. Tube: Aldgate East.*

In among a glut of similar establishments, the quality of the cuisine—fresh ingredients, big portions—has made **10** ★★ **Aladin** the unofficial king of the local curry house scene. *132 Brick Lane.* ☎ *020/7247-8210. www.aladinbricklane.co.uk. £.*

Whitehall

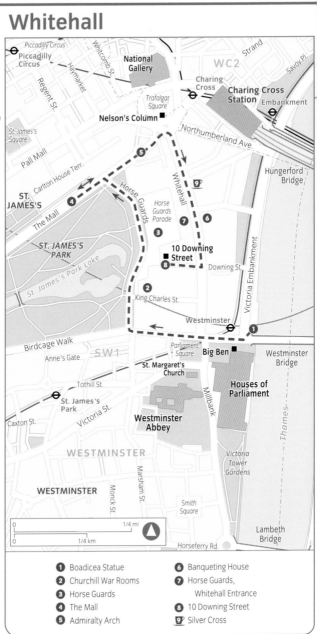

1 Boadicea Statue	**6** Banqueting House	
2 Churchill War Rooms	**7** Horse Guards,	
3 Horse Guards		Whitehall Entrance
4 The Mall	**8** 10 Downing Street	
5 Admiralty Arch	**9** Silver Cross	

Once the site of the vast Palace of Whitehall—London's chief royal residence from 1530 to 1698—this area is now a dignified neighborhood of government buildings whose grand architecture confers a certain beauty to the dull business of bureaucracy. This walk is best in the morning; time to arrive at Horse Guards Parade to see the Changing of the Guard. START: **Westminster Tube Station.**

1 Boadicea Statue. A tall and ferocious queen of the Iceni tribe of East Anglia, Boadicea waged battle against Britain's 1st-century Roman invaders, nailing captured soldiers to trees and flaying them alive. In A.D. 61, her forces temporarily retook Londinium before they were thoroughly defeated by the Roman army. The queen (whose name means victorious) became a heroic figure of Victorian England. This statue by Thomas Thornycroft was erected in 1902. *Bridge St. & Victoria Embankment.*

2 ★★ kids Churchill War Rooms. Winston Churchill directed World War II from this underground shelter as German bombs rained down on London. The basements of these Civil Service buildings were redesigned in the war to house a hospital, a cafeteria, sleeping quarters, and even a shooting range. After the war, the area was locked and left untouched until Churchill's quarters were turned into a museum in 1981; all the items you see are the genuine article. ⏱ *1 hr. Clive Steps, King Charles St.* ☎ *020/7930-6961. http://cwr.iwm. org.uk. Adults £15.95, children free. Daily 9:30am–6pm.*

3 ★★ kids Horse Guards. This grand 18th-century building is the headquarters of the Household Cavalry Mounted Regiment, the chief bodyguards of the Queen. At the small on-site museum, you can see members tending to their horses in the adjacent stables, through a glass partition. The large parade ground out front is the site for the annual **Trooping the Colour** ceremony. Every day at 11am (10am on Sun) there's a much mellower (and less crowded) Changing of the Guard than you'll find at Buckingham Palace (p 21, **3**). ⏱ *45 min. Horse Guards Rd. Household Cavalry Museum:* ☎ *020/7930-3070. www. householdcavalrymuseum.co.uk. Adults £6, children 5–16 £4. Daily 10am–5pm.*

4 The Mall. This red-gravel thoroughfare—running west from Buckingham Palace (p 35, **1**) to Trafalgar Square (p 22, **5**)—was created in 1660 as a venue for St. James's gallants to play the popular game of *paille mall* (a precursor to croquet). In the early 18th century it was a fashionable promenade for the beau monde, and in 1903 it was redesigned as a processional route for royal occasions. When foreign heads of state visit the queen, the Mall is decked out in the Union Jack and the flags of the visitor's country. *Between Buckingham Palace & Admiralty Arch.*

5 ★ Admiralty Arch. Built in 1910, this quintuple-arched building looks west to the grand statue of Queen Victoria in front of Buckingham Palace. The central gates are for ceremonial use, opening only to let a royal procession pass. Note the adorable little ships sitting atop some of the nearby street lamps in a nod to the Old Admiralty Offices for which the arch was named.

6 ★★★ **Banqueting House.** All that remains of Whitehall Palace is this hall, completed in 1622 by Inigo Jones. The city's first Renaissance-style construction is best known for its glorious Rubens-painted ceiling—commissioned by Charles I (1600–49), who used the building for parties and greeting foreign delegations. The allegorical painting, equating the Stuart kings with the gods, may have gone to Charles's head—his belief in the divine right of kings led directly to his execution for treason in 1649 just outside the hall. *Whitehall.* 🕐 *30 min.* ☎ *0844/ 482-7777. www.hrp.org.uk/ banquetinghouse/. Adults £5, seniors £4, children 15 & under free. Mon–Sat 10am–5pm.*

7 **Horse Guards, Whitehall Entrance.** Just across from the Banqueting House is another entrance to Horse Guards Parade guarded by two mounted soldiers in ceremonial garb who provide good photo opportunities for visitors. Go through the gates and have a look through the arched tunnel, framing a beautiful view of St. James's Park.

8 **10 Downing Street.** The home address of Britain's prime minister since 1732 is set in a quiet cul-de-sac blocked off by iron gates for security reasons. There's not much to see now except a lot of police giving you the evil eye, though there is a *frisson* of excitement to be had while standing near so much power.

Of the many fine pubs in Whitehall, one of the best is the **9** **Silver Cross,** which, despite its faux ye olde England decor, is genuinely old (it was granted a brothel license in 1674). It offers good fish and chips, lots of seating, and its own ghost—a young girl in Tudor dress. *33 Whitehall.* ☎ *020/7930-8350. ££.* ●

The ceiling at Banqueting House was painted by Rubens.

4 The Best Shopping

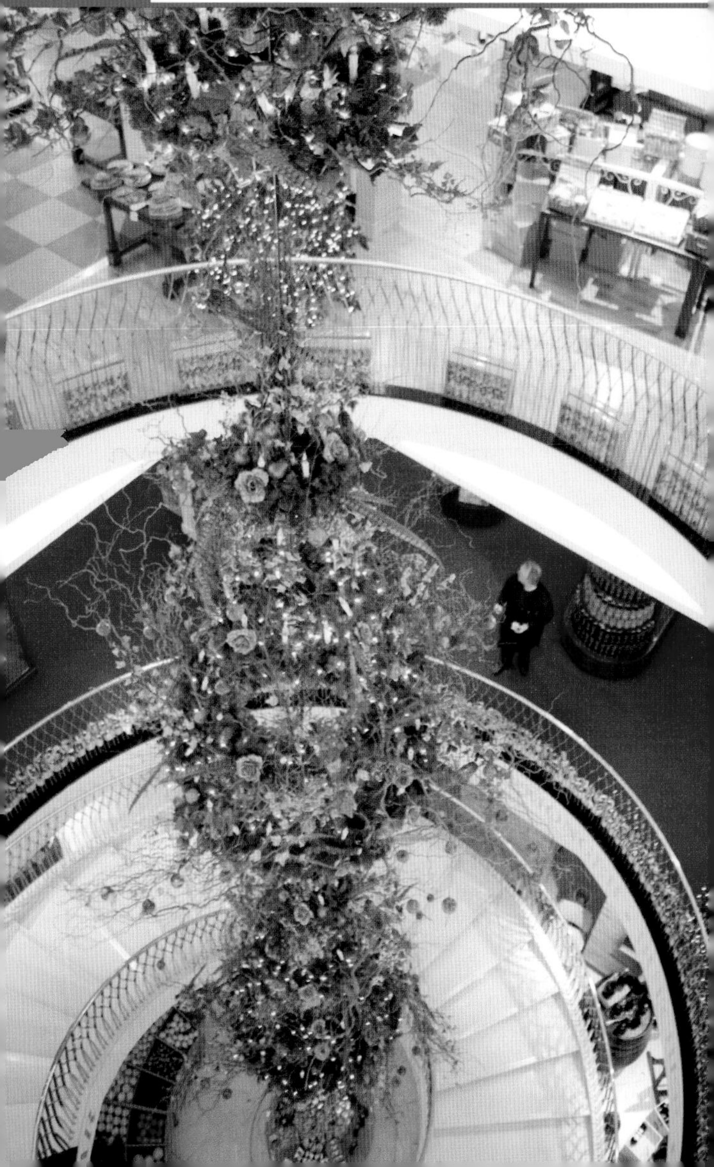

Shopping Best Bets

Head to Borough Market for lunchtime.

Best **Time to Shop**
During the August and January
citywide, month-long sales

Best **Shot at Last Season's
Designer Threads**
★★ Pandora, *16–22 Cheval Place
(p 81)*

Best **High-End Jewelry**
★★★ Ritz Fine Jewellery, *150 Piccadilly (p 84)*

Best **Fun & Vintage Jewelry**
★★ Hirst Antiques, *59 Pembridge
Rd. (p 84)*

Best **Sugar Rush**
★★ Artisan du Chocolat, *89 Lower
Sloane St. (p 82)*

Best **Children's Toy Store**
★ Honey Jam, *2 Blenheim Crescent.
(p 86)*

Best Place to **Score Stuff from
Other People's Attics**
★★★ Grays Antique Market, *58
Davies St. (p 78)*

Best **Foot Forward**
★ The Natural Shoe Store, *13 Neal
St. (p 81)*

Previous page: Fortnum & Mason.

Best Place to **Find Out Where
You Are**
★★★ Stanfords, *12–14 Long Acre
(p 79)*

Best **Hot-Date Lingerie**
★★ Agent Provocateur, *6 Broadwick St. (p 84)*

Best for **Free Tastings**
★★★ Borough Market, *Southwark
St. (p 82)*

Most **Fun Auction House**
★★ Auction Atrium, *101b Kensington Church St. (p 78)*

Best of **All Worlds**
★★ The General Trading Company,
91 Pelham Street. (p 83)

Best **Weekend Browsing**
★★★ Portobello Road Market,
Portobello Rd. (p 85)

Best **Everything**
★★★ Selfridges, *400 Oxford St.
(p 81)*

Best **Museum Shop**
★★★ Victoria & Albert Museum,
Cromwell Rd. (p 85)

Best **Parfumerie**
★★ Angela Flanders, *96 Columbia
Rd. (p 78)*

Chelsea & Knightsbridge
Shopping

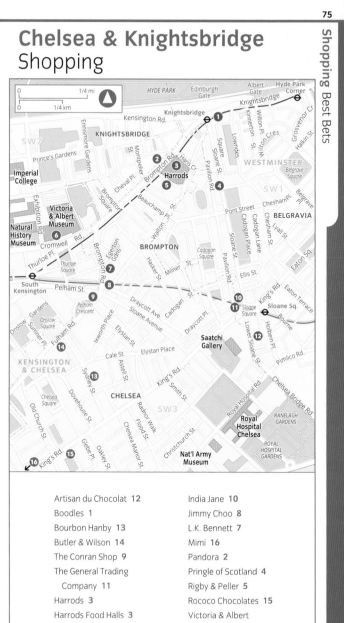

Artisan du Chocolat **12**

Boodles **1**

Bourbon Hanby **13**

Butler & Wilson **14**

The Conran Shop **9**

The General Trading
  Company **11**

Harrods **3**

Harrods Food Halls **3**

Harrods Toy Kingdom **3**

India Jane **10**

Jimmy Choo **8**

L.K. Bennett **7**

Mimi **16**

Pandora **2**

Pringle of Scotland **4**

Rigby & Peller **5**

Rococo Chocolates **15**

Victoria & Albert
  Museum **6**

Central London Shopping

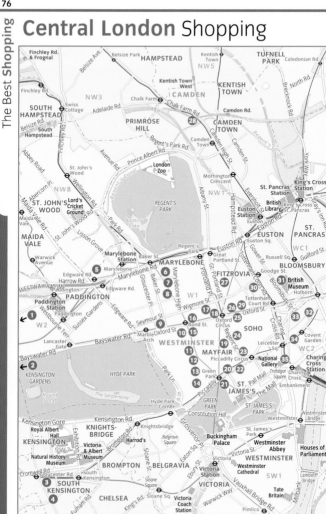

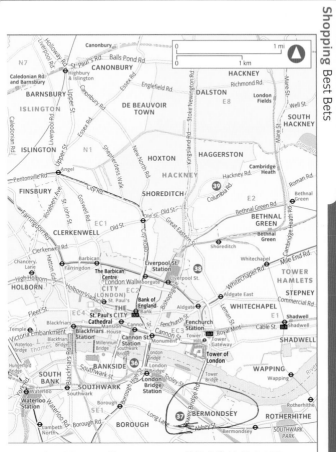

Geo. F. Trumper **13**	Old Spitalfields Market **38**
Gloucester Road Book Store **3**	Ottolenghi **2**
Graham & Green **1**	Portobello Road Market **2**
Grays Antique Market **10**	The Print Gallery Art Shop **2**
Hamleys **24**	Ritz Fine Jewellery **21**
Hirst Antiques **2**	Screen Face **32**
Honey Jam **2**	Selfridges **16**
John Lewis **18**	Smythson of Bond Street **11**
La Senza **29**	Space NK **1**
Lush **23**	Stanfords **34**
Marks & Spencer **9**	Summerill & Bishop **2**
Miller Harris **12**	Talking Book Shop **17**
National Gallery Gift Shop **35**	Topshop **26**
The Natural Shoe Store **33**	Villandry **27**
New Look **25**	Waterstone's **22**

London Shopping A to Z

Antiques & Art Auctions

★★★ Alfie's Antique Market

MARYLEBONE   The city's largest indoor antique market—four floors of secondhand knickknacks, plus old fabrics and dresses. *13–25 Church St. ☎ 020/7723-6066. www.alfies antiques.com. Some dealers take credit cards. Tube: Marylebone. Map p 76.*

★★ Arieta Decorative Arts

KENSINGTON   Tiny and charming, this wonderful curio shop is the rare store where you'll find something unusual that won't blow your budget. *97b Kensington Church St. ☎ 020/7243-1074. MC, V. Tube: Notting Hill Gate. Map p 76.*

★★ Auction Atrium KENSINGTON

A user-friendly bidding website, Auction Atrium offers affordable estate sales and the richly filled walk-in shop has lots of buy-now items at good prices. It's much more fun than the big auction houses. *101b Kensington Church St. ☎ 020/7792-9020. www. auctionatrium.com. AE, MC, V. Tube: Notting Hill Gate. Map p 76.*

★ Bermondsey (New Caledonian) Market BERMONDSEY   Join

the crush of dealers fighting over the estate goods and antiques sold here from 4am on a Friday. Stalls are pretty much all packed up and gone by 11am. *Corner of Bermondsey St. & Long Lane. ☎ 020/7969-1500. Some dealers take credit cards. Tube: Bermondsey. Map p 76.*

★ Bourbon Hanby CHELSEA   A

rather grand collection of antiques stalls featuring upscale estate goods, jewelry, and fine art. *151 Sydney St. ☎ 020/7352-2106. www. bourbonhanby.com. Some dealers take credit cards. Tube: Sloane Sq. Map p 75.*

★★ Christie's SOUTH KENSING-

TON   Don't be scared off by the cost of the serious treasures—this venerable auction house usually has something for all budgets. *85 Old Brompton Rd. ☎ 020/7930-6074. www.christies.com. AE, MC, V. Tube: S. Kensington. Map p 76.*

★★★ Grays Antique Market

MAYFAIR   Stalls here sell everything from Art Deco paperweights and antique jewelry to vintage Edwardian toys. *58 Davies St. ☎ 020/ 7629-7034. www.graysantiques.com. Some dealers take credit cards. Tube: Bond St., Marble Arch. Map p 76.*

Beauty Products

★★ Angela Flanders EAST END

This exclusive shop is well worth the effort it takes to get to the East End on a Sunday between 10am and 3pm (or by appointment). Flanders' bespoke, signature scents have a devoted clientele. *96 Columbia Rd.*

Alfie's Antique Market.

☎ 020/7739-7555. www.angela flanders-perfumer.com. AE, MC, V. Tube: Old St. Map p 76.

★★ Geo. F. Trumper MAYFAIR An essential shop for the well-groomed man, the woman who wants a great gift for her guy, or anyone interested in high-quality toiletries and shaving accessories. 9 Curzon St. ☎ 020/7499-1850. www. trumpers.com. AE, MC, V. Tube: Gloucester Rd. Map p 76.

Lush MAYFAIR There's no missing a branch of this popular British chain—not if you have a sense of smell, anyway—as the fruity, heady scents of their "all natural" soaps, bath oils, and cosmetics do tend to pervade the surrounding area. Great for gifts. 80–82 Regent St. ☎ 020/7434-3953. www.lush.co.uk. MC, V. Tube: Piccadilly Circus. Map p 76.

★★ Miller Harris MAYFAIR Trained in Grasse, France, Lyn Harris has created a global brand of sexy and elegant scents of the finest quality, as well as beautifully packaged lotions and candles. 21 Bruton St. ☎ 020/7629-7750. www.miller harris.com. AE, DC, MC, V. Tube: Green Park or Bond St. Map p 76.

★★ Screen Face COVENT GARDEN Even if you're not in the market for a special-effects bruise kit, you'll be knocked out by the range and variety of makeup, accessories, and skin goods at this favorite of pro makeup artists. 48 Monmouth St. ☎ 020/7836-3955. www.screenface. co.uk. MC, V. Tube: Covent Garden. Map p 76.

★ Space NK NOTTING HILL This popular British chain sells many boutique-style lines of makeup, creams, fragrances, and decadently scented candles. 127–131 Westbourne Grove. ☎ 020/7727-8063. www.spacenk.co.uk. MC, V. Tube: Notting Hill Gate. Map p 76.

Books & Stationery

★★★ Daunt Books MARYLEBONE One of the few stores left of this small chain. There is an excellent travel section and the latest U.K. fiction. There's a peaceful atmosphere for browsing. 183 Marylebone High St. ☎ 020/7224-2295. www.daunt books.co.uk. MC, V. Tube: Baker St. Map p 76.

★★ Gloucester Road Book Store KENSINGTON Good prices on secondhand books (£3–£4 for paperback fiction) that have been carefully sourced by the knowledgeable staff. Check out the coffee mugs imprinted with old Penguin book covers. 123 Gloucester Rd. ☎ 020/7370-3503. MC, V. Tube: Gloucester Rd. Map p 76.

★★ Smythson of Bond Street MAYFAIR This expensive and exclusive stationer caters to generations of posh Londoners, who would feel naked without a Smythson appointment diary. 40 New Bond St. ☎ 020/7629-8558. www.smythson. com. AE, MC, V. Tube: Bond St. Map p 76.

★★★ Stanfords COVENT GARDEN The destination for all disoriented travelers (providing you find your way here, of course), Stanfords is London's largest guidebook and map store. If you can't find a guide to it here, it probably hasn't been discovered yet. 12–14 Long Acre. ☎ 020/7836-1321. www.stanfords. co.uk. MC, V. Tube: Covent Garden. Map p 76.

★ Talking Book Shop MARYLEBONE Gob-smacking selection of audio books (London's largest) including fiction, biography, history, self-help, and more on MP3, CD, or, if you're feeling old-school, cassette. 36 Baker St. ☎ 020/7486-7040. www.talkingbooks.co.uk. MC, V. Tube: Bond St. Map p 76.

★★ **Waterstone's** PICCADILLY
The flagship branch of the U.K.'s
leading book chain takes up five
floors, making it Europe's largest
bookstore. The choice is enormous.
The top floor has a restaurant and
stunning views of London. *203–206
Piccadilly.* ☎ *020/7851-2400. www.
waterstones.com. MC, V. Tube: Piccadilly Circus. Map p 76.*

Clothing & Shoes
★★ **The Antique Clothing Shop**
NOTTING HILL   Lots of great old glad
rags, plus work get-ups from your
great-grandmother's day. *282 Portobello Rd.* ☎ *020/8964-4830. AE.
Tube: Ladbroke Grove. Map p 76.*

★★ **Bang Bang** FITZROVIA   This
women's clothing exchange offers
you the chance to pick up some
cheap designer gear—vintage or
recent—for cash or as a direct
swap. But be warned if you're hoping to exchange: The staff have very
discerning tastes, so bring your
wallet just in case. *21 Goodge St.*
☎ *020/7631-4191. MC, V. Tube:
Goodge St. Map p 76.*

★ **Browns** MAYFAIR   The best
place in town for up-to-the-minute

fashions, including a discriminating
collection of hip designers. It's
expensive, so keep your eyes peeled
for sales. *24–27 S. Moulton St.*
☎ *020/7514-0016. www.browns-
fashion.com. AE, DC, MC, V. Tube:
Bond St. Map p 76.*

★★ **Catwalk** MARYLEBONE
There's always an excellent chance
of getting some designer clothes
and shoes at this "nearly new" shop,
crammed with top labels that are
priced to move. *52 Blandford St.*
☎ *020/7935-1052. MC, V. Tube:
Baker St. Map p 76.*

★★ **The Cross** HOLLAND PARK
Fashionistas in the know flock here
for Missoni, Johnny Loves Rosie,
Alice Lee, and other designers. You'll
also find housewares and surprisingly witty children's gifts. *141 Portland Rd.* ☎ *020/7727-6760. AE, MC,
V. Tube: Holland Park. Map p 76.*

★★ **Dover Street Market** MAY-
FAIR   Resoundingly and expen-
sively cutting edge, the DSM
encompasses four floors of top fashion: Commes des Garçons (the main
brand) shares space with Azzedine
Alaïa, and the latest catwalk stars.
17–18 Dover St. ☎ *020/7518-0680.*

Designer fashion at Browns.

www.doverstreetmarket.com. AE, MC, V. Tube: Green Park. Map p 76.

★★ Jimmy Choo SOUTH KENSINGTON   The London-based global brand pops up on the well-tended feet of Oscar contenders and well-kept mistresses. You'll pay dearly for a pair. *32 Sloane St. ☎ 020/7823-1051. www.jimmychoo.com. AE, MC, V. Tube: Knightsbridge. Map p 75.*

★ L.K. Bennett SOUTH KENSINGTON   Leave the clothes on the racks, but do step into the shoes. Boots are plentiful, and there are plenty of dressy flats and come-hither pumps for the demure-shoe freak. *39–41 Brompton Rd. ☎ 020/7225-1916. www.lkbennett.com. AE, DC, MC, V. Tube: Knightsbridge. Map p 75.*

★★ Mimi CHELSEA   This little boutique carries clothes and accessories from trendsetters. Alice Temperley, Issa London, Queen and Belle, and others. *309 King's Rd. ☎ 020/7349-9699. www.mimilondon.co.uk. AE, MC, V. Tube: Sloane Sq., then bus no. 11. Map p 75.*

★ The Natural Shoe Store COVENT GARDEN   Come here for the best of Birkenstock, Josef Seibel, Arche, and other comfortable hippie styles now totally in vogue. *13 Neal St. ☎ 020/7836-5254. www.thenaturalshoestore.com. AE, MC, V. Tube: Covent Garden. Map p 76.*

★ New Look SOHO   One of the giants of the affordable women's fashion scene, New Look's strength is its dependability. The clothes may be cheap, but they're usually durable enough to last the season—if not beyond—unlike those of many of its competitors. *203 Oxford St. ☎ 020/7851-7360. www.newlook.com. AE, MC, V. Tube: Oxford Circus. Map p 76.*

★★ Pandora KNIGHTSBRIDGE   A big, well-organized shop featuring lots of designer names, shoes, and accessories previously owned by frightfully fashionable Knightsbridge clotheshorses. *16–22 Cheval Place. ☎ 020/7589-5289. www.pandoradressagency.com. AE, MC, V. Tube: Knightsbridge. Map p 75.*

Pringle of Scotland CHELSEA Putting its reputation for cheesy golf cardigans behind it, this luxury retailer now sells an assortment of dressy casual-wear and woolens that are very much up to the minute. *141 Sloane St. ☎ 020/7881-3060. www.pringlescotland.com. AE, DC, MC, V. Tube: Sloane Sq. Map p 75.*

★★ Topshop MARYLEBONE   An absolute must-go for the younger generation, but even older women find something to love in this mecca of street fashion at decent prices. The flagship shop on Oxford Circus is a madhouse, but has the widest range of items. *Oxford Circus. ☎ 0844/848-7847. www.topshop.com. AE, MC, V. Tube: Oxford Circus. Map p 76.*

Department Stores

★ Harrods KNIGHTSBRIDGE   From its food halls to its home entertainment centers, Harrods is a London institution—as well as an overhyped and overpriced bore. *87–135 Brompton Rd. ☎ 020/7730-234. www.harrods.com. AE, DC, MC, V. Tube: Knightsbridge. Map p 75.*

★★★ John Lewis MARYLEBONE This is *the* place to find homey necessities such as sewing notions, fabrics, and kitchenware. Londoners can't live without it. *278–306 Oxford St. ☎ 020/7629-7711. www.johnlewis.co.uk. AE, DC, MC, V. Tube: Oxford Circus. Map p 76.*

★★★ Selfridges MARYLEBONE Inside and out, this grand old department store is the best in town. The food halls are great, as

Harrods, purveyor of luxury goods.

are the fashions; it even offers tattooing and piercing. *400 Oxford St. ☎ 0800/123-400. www.selfridges. com. AE, DC, MC, V. Tube: Marble Arch. Map p 76.*

Food & Chocolates

★★ **Artisan du Chocolat** CHELSEA   This award-winning shop creates quirky and delicious flavored chocolates and truffles for the connoisseur. Try the lavender chocolate—close your eyes, and you'll be in Provence. *89 Lower Sloane St. ☎ 020/7824-8365. www.artisanduchocolat.com. MC, V. Tube: Sloane Sq. Map p 75.*

★★★ **Borough Market** BANKSIDE   This is a gourmet paradise, with stalls piled high with free-range meats, fruit and veg, and homemade produce. But London's finest food market can be both mouthwateringly delicious and eye-wateringly expensive—unless you restrict yourself to free samples. Open Thursday to Saturday. *Southwark St. ☎ 020/ 7407-1002. www.boroughmarket. org.uk. Tube: London Bridge. Map p 76.*

★★ **Fortnum & Mason** MAYFAIR The city's ultimate grocer stocks goodies fit for the queen—or friends back home—plus gourmet

picnic fare and specialty teas. *181 Piccadilly. ☎ 020/7734-8040. www. fortnumandmason.com. AE, DC, MC, V. Tube: Green Park. Map p 76.*

★★ **Harrods Food Halls** KNIGHTSBRIDGE   Harrods sells loads of edible gifts branded with its famous name; be sure to ogle the remarkable ceilings in the produce and meat sections. *87–135 Brompton Rd. ☎ 020/7730-1234. www. harrods.com. AE, DC, MC, V. Tube: Knightsbridge. Map p 75.*

★★★ **Ottolenghi** KENSINGTON This small shop is filled with exquisite European desserts—English puddings, French gâteaux, Italian *tortas*, German *bundts*—in every form and flavor. *Holland St. ☎ 020/ 7937-0003. www.ottolenghi.co.uk. MC, V. Tube: Kensington High St. Map p 76.*

★★ **Rococo Chocolates** CHELSEA   Chocoholics love this fine store, which stocks wittily shaped, high-cocoa-content confections and unique flavors (Earl Grey, rose, and more). *321 King's Rd. ☎ 020/7352-5857. www.rococochocolates.com. MC, V. Tube: Sloane Sq., then bus no. 11. Map p 75.*

★ **Villandry** MARYLEBONE Hearty foodstuffs are displayed in a pleasing setting, and there's also a cafe and restaurant. *170 Great Portland St.* ☎ *020/7631-3131. www.villandry.com. AE, DC, MC, V. Tube: Great Portland St. Map p 76.*

Home Decor

Cologne & Cotton MARYLEBONE Stock up here on elegant bed clothes of pure linen, and cotton sheets in soothing colors and simple designs. The pillowcases are gorgeous, and come in all sizes. *88 Marylebone High St.* ☎ *020/7486-0595. www.cologneandcotton.com. MC, V. Tube: Baker St. Map p 76.*

★★ The Conran Shop SOUTH KENSINGTON Your best bets among the large and varied selection of high-priced merchandise here are the kitchenware and bath items. *Michelin House, 81 Fulham Rd.* ☎ *020/7589-7401. www.conranshop.co.uk. AE, MC, V. Tube: S. Kensington. Map p 75.*

★★ The General Trading Company CHELSEA Started in the 1920s, this shop sells useful as well as merely charming household goods and clever knickknacks from all over the world. *91 Pelham St.*

Beautifully wrapped Rococo Chocolates.

☎ *020/7225-6740. www.general-trading.co.uk. AE, MC, V. Tube: S. Kensington. Map p 75.*

Graham & Green NOTTING HILL Lighting, stationery, and attractive home-decor whatnots fill Graham & Green's charming little shop, just off Portobello Road. *4 & 10 Elgin Crescent.* ☎ *020/7243-8908. www.grahamandgreen.co.uk. AE, MC, V. Tube: Notting Hill. Map p 76.*

Royal fare at Fortnum & Mason.

★ **India Jane** CHELSEA This store gathers the best of India's most dignified furnishings and decor, and sells well-priced knickknacks and bibelots. *121 King's Rd.* ☎ *020/7351-9940. www.indiajane.co.uk. AE, MC, V. Tube: Sloane Sq. Map p 75.*

★★ **Summerill & Bishop** HOLLAND PARK Shop here for a sumptuous collection of French housewares, from efficient, humble radiator dusters to the finest table settings and cookery items. *100 Portland St.* ☎ *020/7221-4566. www.summerillandbishop.com. MC, V. Tube: Holland Park. Map p 76.*

Jewelry

★ **Boodles** KNIGHTSBRIDGE One of England's oldest jewelers (opened in 1798), Boodles has resident designers who keep its collection fresh and modern (not to mention expensive). *1 Sloane St.* ☎ *020/7235-0111. www.boodles.com. AE, DC, MC, V. Tube: Knightsbridge. Map p 75.*

Butler & Wilson SOUTH KENSINGTON You won't have to remortgage your house to buy the beautiful costume and silver jewelry here. It's *the* best shop in town for tiaras. *189 Fulham Rd.* ☎ *020/7352-8255. www.butlerandwilson.co.uk. AE, MC, V. Tube: S. Kensington. Map p 75.*

★★ **Hirst Antiques** NOTTING HILL Something of a jewelry museum, here you'll find extravagant vintage costume baubles from European catwalks of yore, and some interesting new gems as well. *59 Pembridge Rd.* ☎ *020/7727-9364. www.hirstantiques.co.uk. MC, V. Tube: Notting Hill Gate. Map p 76.*

★★★ **Ritz Fine Jewellery** ST. JAMES Arguably the best hotel jewelry shop in the world, thanks to its collections of well-set semiprecious gems and serious rocks. Of course, when the hotel is the Ritz, it had better be the best. *150 Piccadilly.* ☎ *020/7409-1312. www.ritzfinejewellery.com. AE, MC, V. Tube: Green Park. Map p 76.*

Lingerie

★★ **Agent Provocateur** SOHO Provocative, indeed! This store's sexy underclothes are works of art. If you've fallen off your diet, however, don't bother walking in as sizes are small. *6 Broadwick St.* ☎ *020/7439-0229. www.agentprovocateur.com. AE, DC, MC, V. Tube: Oxford Circus. Map p 76.*

★ **La Senza** FITZROVIA Come here for classy, well-priced lingerie; some of the bras are almost too beautiful to hide beneath clothing. *162 Oxford St.* ☎ *020/7636-8173. www.lasenza.co.uk. AE, DC, MC, V. Tube: Oxford Circus. Map p 76.*

★★ **Marks & Spencer** MARYLEBONE This beloved, reliable outlet for comfy cotton underwear for men and women has kept up with the times, and offers a lot more than old-lady knickers. *458 Oxford St.* ☎ *020/7935-7954. www.marksandspencer.com. AE, DC, MC, V. Tube: Marble Arch. Map p 76.*

★ **Rigby & Peller** KNIGHTSBRIDGE The corsetiere to the queen specializes in classy underwear, bathing suits (ask for "swimming costumes"), and finely engineered brassieres. *2 Hans Rd.* ☎ *0845/076-5545. www.rigbyandpeller.com. AE, DC, MC, V. Tube: Knightsbridge. Map p 75.*

Markets

★★★ **Camden Market** CAMDEN TOWN It may promote itself as the "capital of alternative London" but this riotous collection of venues (there's no one Camden Market, but rather several stretching along the

Camden Market.

high street), selling arts, crafts, jewelry, vintage fashion, club wear, food, and more, is now one of the capital's top tourist attractions, putting it at the heart of the mainstream. *Camden High St.* ☎ *020/ 7974-6767. www.camdenlock.net. Tube: Camden Town. Map p 76.*

★★ Old Spitalfields Market

SHOREDITCH   Head to Spitalfields' huge indoor market on Sunday for organic produce, ethnic clothes, knickknacks, and handmade crafts. *Commercial St.* ☎ *020/7247-8556. Most dealers take cash only. www. visitspitalfields.com. Tube: Liverpool St. Map p 76.*

★★★ Portobello Road Market

NOTTING HILL   Saturday is the best day to join the throngs at Portobello's famous antiques market, although you can also find fashion, secondhand goods and fruit and veg. Bring cash. *Portobello Rd. (from Notting Hill end to Ladbroke Grove). Some dealers take credit cards. www.portobelloroad.co.uk. Tube: Notting Hill. Map p 76.*

Museum Shops
★ kids British Museum BLOOMS-BURY   The B.M. has four shops: A bookshop, a "family" shop, a

"collection" shop (selling souvenirs), and a "culture" shop (stocked with luxury items, many based on items in the museum's collection). *Great Russell St.* ☎ *020/7323-8000. www. thebritishmuseumshoponline.org. AE, DC, MC, V. Tube: Russell Sq. Map p 76.*

★★ National Gallery Gift Shop

WEST END   This is the city's best source for art-related books and stationery. A "print on demand" service allows you to purchase a copy of any picture in the collection. *Trafalgar Sq.* ☎ *020/7747-2870. www. nationalgallery.org.uk. AE, DC, MC, V. Tube: Charing Cross. Map p 76.*

★★★ kids Victoria & Albert
Museum SOUTH KENSINGTON   This must-stop shop sells everything from postcards to jewelry. Cool finds include hand-painted tools and nostalgic toys. *Cromwell Rd.* ☎ *020/7942-2000. www.vam.ac.uk. AE, DC, MC, V. Tube: S. Kensington. Map p 75.*

Toys
★ kids Hamleys PICCADILLY   London's most famous toy store has seven floors of toys, games, tricks, dolls, and more. As you enter the

The Best Shopping

Paddington Bear at Hamleys toy shop.

store, you are greeted by a giant array of (often giant-size) cuddly toys. *189–196 Regent St.* ☎ *0871/704-1977. www.hamleys.com. AE, DC, MC, V. Tube: Oxford Circus. Map p 76.*

★ kids **Harrods Toy Kingdom**
KNIGHTSBRIDGE   There is something here for all ages, plus kiddie-size cars and life-size stuffed animals. Be prepared for a bad case of the "gimmes" from your kids. *4th Floor, 87–135 Brompton Rd.* ☎ *020/7730-1234. www.harrods.com. AE, DC, MC, V. Tube: Knightsbridge. Map p 75.*

★ kids **Honey Jam** NOTTING HILL
Created by two mums, this fabulously fun and on-target toy shop sells fine toys from Europe and crazy little gimcracks for party bags. There's also a small selection of adorable clothes. *2 Blenheim Crescent.* ☎ *020/7243-0449. www.honeyjam.co.uk. MC, V. Tube: Ladbroke Grove. Map p 76.*

★ kids **The Print Gallery Art Shop** KENSINGTON   For creative kids and grown-ups, the craft kits and materials in this crammed-full shop are sourced from all over Europe. *22 Pembridge Rd.* ☎ *020/7221-8885. AE, DC, MC, V. Tube: Notting Hill Gate. Map p 76.* ●

VAT (Value Added Tax)

The U.K. levies a crushing 20% Value Added Tax (VAT) on all non-essential goods. (VAT is usually included in the price tag, unless it clearly states "plus VAT.") If you live outside the EU, you can apply to have your VAT refunded. Most shops will help you if you spend a certain amount, usually at least £50. Ask for a VAT form when you pay and have it filled out in the shop—forms must be validated by the seller. When you get to the airport, present your form, passport, and purchases—do not pack them in your checked luggage—to the Customs agency for certification. Once your papers have been stamped, you can get a cash refund from one of the agencies at the airport (minus a service charge), or you can mail in the forms to get a cash or credit card refund. The process is only worth going through for high-ticket items. For more information, go to **www.direct.gov.uk** or **www.visitbritain.com**.

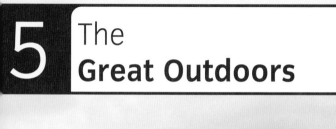

Hyde **Park**

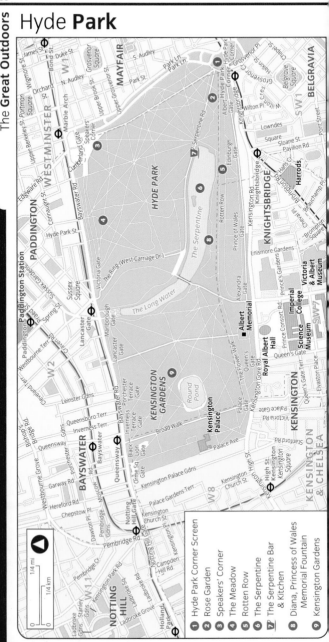

1 Hyde Park Corner Screen
2 Rose Garden
3 Speakers' Corner
4 The Meadow
5 Rotten Row
6 The Serpentine
7 The Serpentine Bar & Kitchen
8 Diana, Princess of Wales Memorial Fountain
9 Kensington Gardens

Previous page: Hampstead Heath.

Since 1536, when Henry VIII appropriated the land from the monks of Westminster Abbey for hunting, 142-hectare (351-acre) Hyde Park has been the scene of duels, highway robbery, and sport. Today, it is a beloved oasis in the midst of the city and in 2012 it will be the venue for the Triathlon and Marathon Swimming events at the London Olympics. START: **Tube to Hyde Park Corner.**

1 Hyde Park Corner Screen. Erected in 1828, this imposing park entrance (one of six) was designed by Decimus Burton, the noted architect responsible for much of Hyde Park's layout. The triple-arched screen is composed of Ionic columns, bronzed ironwork, and carved friezes inspired by the Elgin Marbles (p 27, **3**). Unfortunately, it's being degraded by air pollution at this busy traffic circle. ⏱ *10 min.*

2 ★ kids Rose Garden. From the Rose Garden, a riot of color in the early summer, you can admire the back of Apsley House, the former home of (and currently a museum dedicated to) the Duke of Wellington. Nearby stands the Wellington Arch, topped by a majestic statue, *Winged Victory,* erected to commemorate the Duke's numerous military triumphs. The garden is filled with fountains and climbing-rose trellises, both much loved by kids. Its central fountain is ringed with benches where you can sit with a picnic lunch, as hopeful sparrows flutter around. ⏱ *20–30 min.*

3 Speakers' Corner. The park's northeast corner provides a peculiarly British tribute to free speech. Since 1872, members of the public have been able to stand here and declaim their heartfelt (and often decidedly odd) opinions on whatever topic they choose—and anyone is allowed to answer back. In the past you might have heard Karl Marx, Lenin, or George Orwell trying to convert the masses. ⏱ *15 min.*

4 ★★ kids The Meadow. Amid all the neatly tended greenery is something a little more real. A 4-hectare (10-acre) section of the park has been turned into a wild meadow, filled with blooming flowers in summer and home to an assortment of creatures, including songbirds, butterflies, and creepy crawlies. Free themed walks are offered in summer. Check the website (www.royalparks.gov.uk/Hyde-Park.aspx) for details. ⏱ *30 min.*

Horse riders on Rotten Row.

The Great Outdoors

5 ★ kids **Rotten Row.** In the late 1680s, William III ordered 300 lamps to be hung from trees along this 1.5-mile riding path—whose name is an English corruption of its original appellation, *Route de Roi* ("King's Road")—in a vain attempt to stop the plague of highwaymen active in the park, and thereby turning it into the first artificially illuminated road in the country. The lamps have now gone, but the path is still used by riders from local stables. If you want to give it a try, contact the **Ross Nye Stables,** 8 Bathurst Mews (☎ 020/7262-3791). 🕐 *1 hr. Just north of the park, opposite Lancaster Gate Tube Station. 1-hr rides start at £60.*

6 ★★★ kids **The Serpentine.** Queen Caroline had the Westbourne River dammed in 1730 to create the Serpentine Lake, upon which she moored two royal yachts. This lovely lake is now the premiere boating spot in London for the masses. Should you venture out on the water, you can choose to go it alone by hiring a pedal boat or rowboats from the Boat House, or take it easy aboard the solar-powered ferry. 🕐 *1 hr. Bluebird Boats Ltd., Serpentine Rd. ☎ 020/7262-1330. Hourly rentals £9 adults, £3 children, £22 family. Mar–Oct 10am–5pm.*

7 ★ kids **The Serpentine Bar & Kitchen** has the best view of the Serpentine in the park, and serves hot meals, sandwiches, and drinks (wine included) that are a cut above the usual park cafeteria cuisine. You're welcome to picnic on the tables outside. *Eastern side of the Serpentine.* ☎ *020/7706-0464. £.*

8 ★ kids **Diana, Princess of Wales Memorial Fountain.** This contemporary granite fountain, located across the Serpentine from the Boat House, was opened by the Queen in July 2004. No less dogged by controversy than the woman who inspired it, the 700-ton, £6.5-million fountain has suffered from flooding, closures, and a slippery bottom. Children, who were meant to splash around happily in its cascading waters, are now restricted to toe-dipping by the omnipresent security guards. 🕐 *20 min. Near the Lido, south of the Serpentine.*

9 ★★★ kids **Kensington Gardens.** Originally a part of Hyde Park, the 111-hectare (274-acre) Kensington Gardens were partitioned into an exclusive preserve of royalty in the 18th century, and

Diana, Princess of Wales Memorial Fountain.

were opened again to the public only in the early 1800s. Originally laid out in Dutch style (emphasizing water, avenues, and topiaries), the attractive gardens are especially popular with families.

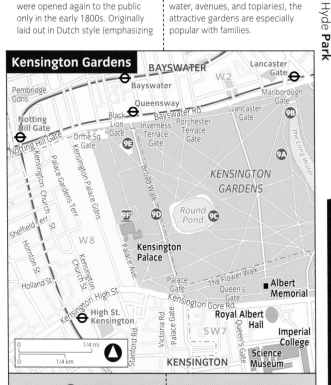

Kensington Gardens

The bronze 9A ★★ kids **Peter Pan Statue** was sculpted in 1912 by Sir George Frampton at the behest of author J. M. Barrie and is the most visited landmark in the park. A short walk north and you'll arrive at 9B ★ kids **The Italian Gardens,** which echoed the rage for all things Italian when it was built in 1861. Generations of children have plied model boats at the 9C ★ kids **Round Pond,** built in 1728. Today you'll also find adults trying out more sophisticated models. West of the pond is the 9D **Broad Walk.** Nineteenth-century ladies and gentlemen promenaded along this tree-lined path past Kensington Palace, and flirted by the nearby bandstand. Kids will race on to the 9E ★★ kids **Diana, Princess of Wales Memorial Playground,** centered on a huge wooden pirate ship. Finish up at Kensington Palace, newly restored and revamped for 2012 (p 37, 7) and a well-earned sit down at the 9F ★★ kids **Orangery Café,** where a very good tea is offered. ⏱ *2–3 hr. Go in the afternoon.* ☎ *0844/482-7777. www.hrp.org.uk/ kensingtonpalace/. Tube: High St. Kensington, Queensway, or Lancaster Gate.*

Regent's **Park**

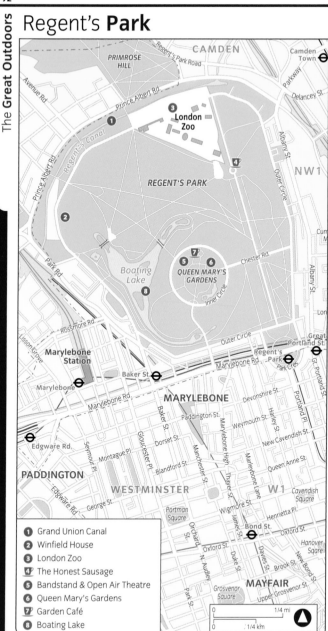

1 Grand Union Canal
2 Winfield House
3 London Zoo
4 The Honest Sausage
5 Bandstand & Open Air Theatre
6 Queen Mary's Gardens
7 Garden Café
8 Boating Lake

This 197-hectare (487-acre) gem started out, like so many parks, as a hunting ground for Henry VIII. It was restyled in the 19th century by John Nash (1752–1835) following the romantic ideal of *rus in urbe* (country in the city). In truth, the sophistication of its flowerbeds, formal gardens with fountains, and ornamental lake make it more *urbe* than *rus*. START: **Tube to Camden Town.**

① ★★ kids **Grand Union Canal.** Londoners traveled the city by boat when Regent's Park was in its infancy, and this is your chance to follow in their wake. The Grand Union Canal, opened in 1814, now covers 137 miles of waterways connecting the river Thames and the Chiltern Hills in Oxfordshire. Water buses ply the scenic Regent's Canal section (opened in 1820) and will take you from Camden Lock's markets through the neighborhoods of colorful houseboats and grand Victorian houses on either side of the canal path in Little Venice—an area whose name is more wishful than accurate (there's just the one canal). Your final destination is the London Zoo inside Regent's Park, for which you can buy slightly discounted combo tickets before getting on the boat. ⏱ *50 min. Camden Lock.*

Jason's tour boat on Regent's Canal.

☎ *020/7482-2550. www.london waterbus.com. One-way tickets £6.90 adults, £5.70 children 3–15. Year-round, depending on the weather.*

② **Winfield House.** As you sail, notice to your left the 4.6-m (15-ft.) high gates protecting a fine mansion beyond. Woolworth heiress Barbara Hutton built this Georgian mansion in 1936, adding extensive gardens and trees. A year after World War II, Hutton donated the antiques-filled home to the American government for use as the official residence of the U.S. ambassador. Unfortunately, you have to be an invited guest to enter.

③ ★★★ kids **London Zoo.** When this former zoology center opened to the public in 1847, many of its captives, such as Jumbo the Elephant (later bought by P. T. Barnum and shipped off to the U.S.), became celebrities. Visitors who complain about the high price of admission might feel differently about this venerable institution if they knew that roughly one-sixth of its 650 species (about 5,000 animals reside here) are endangered—and that the zoo's world-renowned breeding program is the only thing preventing their extinction. Highlights include "Gorilla Kingdom," a moated island resembling an African forest clearing that provides a naturalistic habitat for gorillas and colobus monkeys. ⏱ *2 hr, longer for families. Outer Circle, Regent's Park.* ☎ *020/7722-3333. www.zsl.org/ zsl-london-zoo. Adults £19.80, £18.30 seniors, £16 children 3–15. Daily 10am–5:30pm.*

A meerkat at London Zoo.

⑥ ★ kids Queen Mary's Gardens. Laid out in the 1930s, these regal gardens lie at the heart of the park's Inner Circle and are a place of enchanting colors, fragrances, and watery vistas. The fabulous and carefully tended Rose Gardens are especially beautiful in spring. ⏱ *30 min. Inner Circle.*

Food kiosks scattered around Regent's Park offer sandwiches and drinks. A less-informal option is the **⑦ ★ Garden Café,** which sells a good variety of salads and sandwiches, as well as wine and beer, which you can enjoy on a lovely terrace. *Queen Mary's Garden, adjacent to Rose Garden.* ☎ *020/7935-5729. £.*

If the smell of frying onions at **④ ★ The Honest Sausage** doesn't whet your appetite, nothing will. The menu features organic and relatively healthy lunch options. Best of all, there's a covered veranda to shelter you from sun and rain. *Broadwalk, Regent's Park.* ☎ *020/7224-3872. www.companyofcooks.com. £.*

⑤ ★★ Bandstand & Open Air Theatre. From late May to early September, these two stages feature alfresco concerts and plays, most notably Shakespearean comedies staged by the English Shakespeare Company. *See p 137.*

⑧ ★★ kids Boating Lake. Operating on a schedule that changes with the weather, the Boathouse rents pedal boats and rowboats you can take out on this picturesque lake. Although the concession is usually closed midweek and in winter, you may be able to go boating on any sunny, warm day—whatever the season, be sure to call ahead. ⏱ *1 hr.* ☎ *020/7724-4069. Open weekends Mar–Nov 11am–6pm. Hourly rentals £6.50 adults, £4.40 children, £20 family.* ●

Regent's Park Boating Lake.

Dining Best Bets

Best for **Keeping Kids Happy**
Rainforest Café *20 Shaftesbury Ave.*
(p 108)

Best **Vegetarian**
★★ Food for Thought *31 Neal St.*
(p 103)

Best **Place for Beef**
★★★ Gaucho Grill *19 Swallow St.*
(p 104)

Best **Self-Service or Take-Out**
★ Whole Foods Market Restaurant
63–97 Kensington High St. (p 109)

Best **Neighborhood Italian**
★★★ The Ark *122 Palace Gardens
Terrace (p 102)*

Best **Afternoon Tea**
★★★ Goring Hotel *Beeston Place*
(p 104)

Best **Menu from Centuries
Past**
★★★ Dinner by Heston Blumen-
thal *66 Knightsbridge (p 103)*

Best **Subterranean Dining
Experience**
★ Café in the Crypt *St. Martin-in-
the-Fields, Duncannon St. (p 102)*

Best **American Noshes**
★★ Automat American Brasserie
33 Dover St. (p 102)

Best **Fish & Chips**
★★★ Geales *2 Farmer St. (p 104)*

Best **Tapas**
★★ Tapas Brindisa *18 Southwark
St. (p 109)*

Best **Olde England Vibe**
★ Rules *35 Maiden Lane (p 108)*

Best **View**
★★ The Portrait *St. Martin's Lane*
(p 107)

Best **Stargazing**
★★ The Ivy *1 West St. (p 105)*

Best **Extravagant**
★★★ Gordon Ramsay *68 Royal
Hospital Rd. (p 104)*

Most **Demented Decor**
★★ Sketch *9 Conduit St. (p 109)*

Best **Fast Food**
★★ Leon *12 Ludgate Circus (p 106)*

Best **French**
★★★ Le Gavroche *43 Upper Brook
St. (p 106)*

Best **Greek**
★★ Halepi *18 Leinster Terrace*
(p 105)

Best **Indian**
★★ Tamarind *20 Queen St. (p 109)*

Most **Carnivorous**
★★★ St. John *26 St. John St. (p 108)*

Café in the Crypt, St. Martin-in-the-Fields.

Previous page: The Ritz Palm Court.

Notting Hill Dining

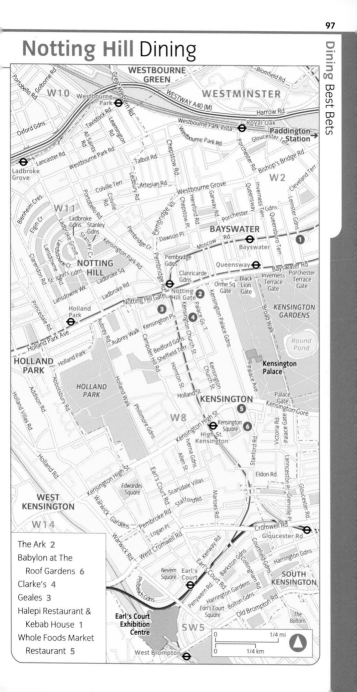

The Ark 2
Babylon at The
Roof Gardens 6
Clarke's 4
Geales 3
Halepi Restaurant &
Kebab House 1
Whole Foods Market
Restaurant 5

Kensington Dining

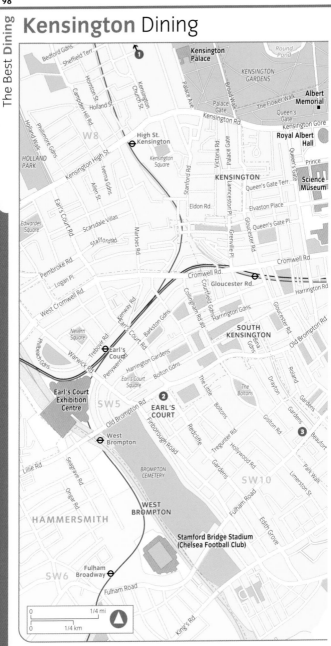

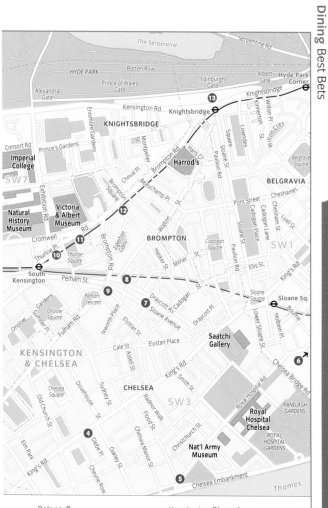

Balans **2**

Bibendum **9**

Café Creperie
of Hampstead **10**

Dinner by
Heston Blumenthal **13**

The Good Earth **12**

Gordon Ramsay **5**

Itsu **8**

Kensington Place **1**

La Poule au Pot **6**

My Old Dutch
Pancake House **4**

Orsini **11**

Poissonnerie
de l'Avenue **7**

Vingt Quatre **3**

West End Dining

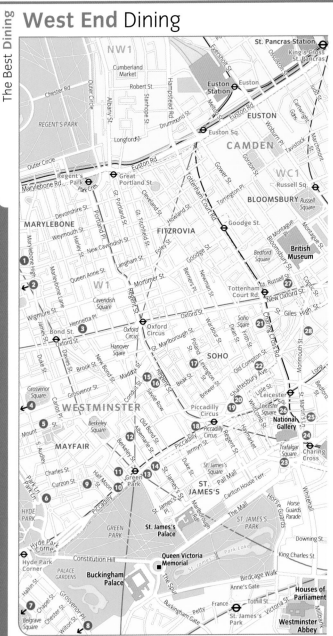

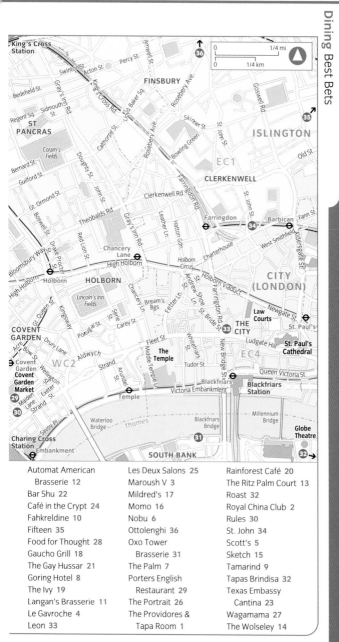

Automat American Brasserie 12	Les Deux Salons 25	Rainforest Café 20
Bar Shu 22	Maroush V 3	The Ritz Palm Court 13
Café in the Crypt 24	Mildred's 17	Roast 32
Fahkreldine 10	Momo 16	Royal China Club 2
Fifteen 35	Nobu 6	Rules 30
Food for Thought 28	Ottolenghi 36	St. John 34
Gaucho Grill 18	Oxo Tower Brasserie 31	Scott's 5
The Gay Hussar 21	The Palm 7	Sketch 15
Goring Hotel 8	Porters English Restaurant 29	Tamarind 9
The Ivy 19	The Portrait 26	Tapas Brindisa 32
Langan's Brasserie 11	The Providores & Tapa Room 1	Texas Embassy Cantina 23
Le Gavroche 4		Wagamama 27
Leon 33		The Wolseley 14

London Restaurants A to Z

★★★ **The Ark** KENSINGTON *ITALIAN* A modest building houses one of the best Italian restaurants in London. Everything is made on the premises, from the fresh pasta to the tiramisu, which is an experience in itself. *122 Palace Gardens Terrace.* ☎ *020/7229-4024. www.ark-restaurant.com. Main course £14–£20. AE, MC, V. Tube: Notting Hill Gate. Map p 97.*

★★ kids **Automat American Brasserie** MAYFAIR *AMERICAN* This elegantly appointed re-creation of a classic diner offers good old Yankee meals for the well-heeled Londoner, and is a little piece of the U.S.A. for homesick visitors. *33 Dover St.* ☎ *020/7499-3033. www.automat-london.com. Main course £8–£32. AE, MC, V. Breakfast, lunch & dinner daily. Tube: Green Park. Map p 100.*

★★ **Babylon at The Roof Gardens** KENSINGTON *MODERN EUROPEAN* Come here on a sunny day to admire the wondrous views from seven floors up, and take advantage of the set lunch prices. *99 Kensington High St. (entrance on Derry St.).* ☎ *020/7368-3993. www.roofgardens. virgin.com. Main course £20–£28. AE, DC, MC, V. Lunch & dinner daily. Tube: High St. Kensington. Map p 97.*

★ kids **Balans** EARLS COURT *INTERNATIONAL* The reasonably priced and varied menu make this a reliable chain for breakfast, lunch, dinner, and, best of all, a wide selection of cocktails. *239 Old Brompton Rd.* ☎ *020/7244-8838. www.balans. co.uk. Main course £10–£23. AE, MC, V. Breakfast, lunch & dinner daily. Tube: Earl's Court. Map p 98.*

★★ **Bar Shu** SOHO *CHINESE* This is super-spicy Szechuan cooking at its best, even if some of the dishes—like braised ox tendons or flash-fried pig's kidneys—may require a leap of faith from the uninitiated. There are plenty of more traditional choices, too. *28 Frith St.* ☎ *020/7287-8822. www.bar-shu. co.uk. Main course £8.90–£28.90. MC, V. Breakfast & lunch daily. Tube: Leicester Sq. Map p 100.*

★★ **Bibendum** SOUTH KENSINGTON *MODERN EUROPEAN* Reliably good food, with an emphasis on fresh fish, and an airy location in the stylish art nouveau Michelin Building make this restaurant an old favorite. *81 Fulham Rd.* ☎ *020/7581-5817. www.bibendum.co.uk. Main course £18–£30. AE, DC, MC, V. Lunch & dinner daily. Tube: S. Kensington. Map p 98.*

kids **Café Creperie of Hampstead** SOUTH KENSINGTON *FRENCH* Treat yourself to one of this authentic French creperie's many savory galettes and sweet crepes. *2 Exhibition Rd.* ☎ *020/7589-8947. Main course £6–£10. MC, V. Lunch & dinner daily. Tube: S. Kensington. Map p 98.*

★ kids **Café in the Crypt** SOHO *BRITISH DINER* This award-winning subterranean cafeteria offers cheap and hearty meals, as well as a jolly good tea. *St. Martin-in-the-Fields, enter on Duncannon St.* ☎ *020/7766-1158. www2.stmartin-in-the-fields. org. Main course £5–£10. MC, V. Breakfast, lunch & dinner daily. Tube: Charing Cross. Map p 100.*

★★★ **Clarke's** KENSINGTON *MODERN EUROPEAN* Chef Sally Clarke gratifies taste buds in her charming dining room, using only the freshest ingredients in her excellent, ever-changing dishes. There's also an on-site shop and bakery. *122 Kensington Church St. ☎ 020/7221-9225. www. sallyclarke.com. Main course £21–£24. AE, DC, MC, V. Lunch & dinner daily. Tube: Notting Hill Gate. Map p 97.*

★★★ **Dinner by Heston Blumenthal** KNIGHTSBRIDGE *TRADITIONAL BRITISH* When Britain's "culinary scientist" Heston Blumenthal serves up traditional British fare, he really means it, with recipes scoured from the history books. Tuck into the charmingly named "Rice & Flesh," (actually calf tail, saffron, and red wine) from 1390, beetroot-flavored porridge from 1660, or spiced pigeon from 1780. Book ahead. *Mandarin Oriental Hyde Park, 66 Knightsbridge. ☎ 020/7201-3833. www.dinnerbyheston.com. Main course £23–£36. AE, DC, MC, V. Lunch & dinner daily. Tube: Knightsbridge. Map p 98.*

★★★ kids **Fakhreldine** MAYFAIR *LEBANESE* London's best Lebanese restaurant, thanks to its

traditional menu, solid service, and fine views of Green Park. *85 Piccadilly. ☎ 020/7493-3424. www. fakhreldine.co.uk. Main course £13–£20. AE, MC, V. Lunch & dinner daily, Sun brunch. Tube: Green Park. Map p 100.*

★★ **Fifteen** HOXTON *ITALIAN* When he's not on one of his various crusades to save us from ourselves, TV's über chef Jamie Oliver presides over this semi-philanthropic venture, which turns disadvantaged youths into chefs. Superior Italian nosh is served in a funky redbrick Victorian building. *14 Westland Place. ☎ 0871/330-1515. www.fifteen.net. Main course £14–£22.50. AE, DC, MC, V. Lunch & dinner daily. Tube: Old St. Map p 100.*

★★ kids **Food for Thought** COVENT GARDEN *VEGETARIAN* Since 1974, this tiny spot has been an underground favorite. The food is fresh, vegetarian, imaginative, and very healthy. *31 Neal St. ☎ 020/7836-0239. http://foodforthought-london. co.uk. Main course £4–£8. No credit cards. Breakfast, lunch & dinner*

Gordon Ramsay's flagship restaurant.

Fish and chips at Porters English Restaurant.

Mon–Sat, lunch Sun. Tube: Covent Garden. Map p 100.

★★★ **kids** **Gaucho Grill** WEST END *ARGENTINEAN*   The best Argentinean dining in Europe, with an emphasis on grilled beef. There's also a small selection of South American wines. *19 Swallow St. ☎ 020/7734-4040. www.gaucho restaurants.co.uk. Main course £14–£39. AE, DC, MC, V. Lunch & dinner daily. Tube: Piccadilly. Map p 100.*

★ **The Gay Hussar** SOHO *HUN-GARIAN*   Since 1953, this tiny dining room has served tasty goulashes, potato pancakes, blini, and other comfort foods to locals and tourists. Try the wild-cherry soup. *2 Greek St. ☎ 020/7437-0973. www.gayhussar. co.uk. Main course £12–£85. MC, V. Lunch & dinner daily. Tube: Totten-ham Court Rd. Map p 100.*

★★★ **Geales** NOTTING HILL *FISH*   Yes, it's got caviar, fresh flowers, linen table cloths, and other posh touches, but go for the humble fish and chips, among the best in London. The sticky toffee pudding is another classic done well. *2 Farmer St. ☎ 020/7727-7528. www.geales. com. Main course £8–£14. AE, MC, V. Lunch & dinner daily. Tube: Not-ting Hill Gate. Map p 97.*

★ **kids** **The Good Earth** KNIGHTS-BRIDGE *CHINESE*   More elegant than your usual Chinese restaurant, with prices to match, this Knights-bridge favorite does a great Beijing duck. It's good for vegetarians, too. *233 Brompton Rd. ☎ 020/7584-3658. Main course £8–£25. AE, MC, V. Lunch & dinner daily. Tube: Knightsbridge. Map p 98.*

★★★ **Gordon Ramsay** CHELSEA *FRENCH*   His restaurant empire may be waning slightly, but the foul-mouthed culinary colossus's flag-ship eatery still has three Michelin stars. *68 Royal Hospital Rd. ☎ 020/ 7352-4441. www.gordonramsay. com. Set lunch £45, dinner £90. AE, DC, MC, V. Lunch & dinner Mon–Fri. Tube: Sloane Sq. Map p 98.*

★★★ **Goring Hotel** VICTORIA *BRITISH*   Mutton broth, steak and kidney pudding, grilled liver, fish galore, and crumble: You can't get more English than the menu at the Goring, a hotel whose dining room and garden recall Edwardian ele-gance at its finest. Afternoon tea is done just right. *Beeston Place. ☎ 020/7396-9000. www.thegoring. com. Set lunch £36–£41, dinner £33–£49, afternoon tea £35–£45. AE, DC, MC, V. Breakfast, lunch & dinner daily. Tube: Victoria. Map p 100.*

★★ **kids** **Halepi Restaurant & Kebab House** BAYSWATER *GREEK* Bring the whole family to share classic home-style Greek dishes and simple Mediterranean-grilled fish and meat. The baklava is the best around. *18 Leinster Terrace.* ☎ *020/7262-1070. www. halepi.co.uk. Main course £12–£22. MC, V. Lunch & dinner daily. Tube: Bayswater. Map p 97.*

kids **Itsu** SOUTH KENSINGTON *ASIAN* A fun, garishly colored place, where diners choose from an excellent selection of small reasonably priced dishes that roll by on a conveyor belt. *118 Draycott Ave.* ☎ *020/7590-2400. www.itsu.com. Main course £5–£12. MC, V. Lunch & dinner daily. Tube: S. Kensington. Map p 98.*

★★ **The Ivy** COVENT GARDEN *MODERN BRITISH* The menu is surprisingly diverse (ranging from caviar to fish cakes to irresistible puddings) at this exclusive haunt of British celebs. For a fancy place, it's not terribly overpriced. *1 West St.* ☎ *020/7836-4751. www.the-ivy. co.uk. Main course £14–£30. AE, DC, MC, V. Lunch & dinner daily. Tube: Leicester Sq. Map p 100.*

★ **Kensington Place** KENSINGTON *MODERN BRITISH* Come here for innovative fresh fish dishes served in a modern, noisy dining room. *201 Kensington Church St.* ☎ *020/7727-3184. www.kensington place-restaurant.co.uk. Set lunch £19.50, dinner £24.50. AE, DC, MC, V. Lunch & dinner daily. Tube: Notting Hill. Map p 98.*

★★ **Langan's Brasserie** ST. JAMES'S *BRASSERIE* A big upscale brasserie with two noisy floors of dining, serving everything from spinach soufflé to fish and chips. *Stratton St.* ☎ *020/7491-8822. www.langansrestaurants.com. Main course £16–£22. AE, DC, MC, V. Lunch & dinner Mon–Sat, lunch Sun. Tube: Green Park. Map p 100.*

★★ **La Poule au Pot** CHELSEA *FRENCH* This chic retro French bistro, much-loved by Londoners, brings a slice of rural France to Chelsea. The cozy atmosphere, friendly staff, and classic dishes always make eating here a joyous occasion. Ask for a large carafe of the house wine. *231 Ebury St.* ☎ *020/7730-7763. www.pouleaupot.co.uk. Main course £18–£24. AE, MC, V. Lunch & dinner daily. Tube: Sloane Square. Map p 98.*

Fantastic views from The Portrait restaurant.

The Best Dining

★★★ **Le Gavroche** MAYFAIR *FRENCH* Internationally renowned Michel Roux Jr. is the chef *patron* of this two-star Michelin extravaganza serving classic French haute cuisine in a clubby, elegant dining room. *43 Upper Brook St.* ☎ *020/7408-0881. www.le-gavroche.co.uk. Set lunch £50, tasting menu £100. AE, DC, MC, V. Lunch & dinner Mon–Fri, dinner Sat. Tube: Marble Arch. Map p 100.*

★★ **Leon** THE CITY *FAST FOOD* Leon combines two seemingly incompatible aims—speedy service and fresh seasonal ingredients—with great success. Top choices include the sweet potato falafel wrap and Moroccan meatballs. *12 Ludgate Circus.* ☎ *020/7489-1580. www.leon restaurants.co.uk. Main course £5.60–£6.25. MC, V. Open 11am–11pm Mon–Fri. Tube: St. Paul's. Map p 100.*

★★ **Les Deux Salons** COVENT GARDEN *FRENCH* You'd expect to find this brasserie on a Parisian backstreet. The interior is a mix of shiny mirrors and dark wood, while the food is expertly prepared. And, just to remind you what country you're in, they also do an afternoon tea for £19.50. *40 William IV St.* ☎ *020/7420-2050. www.lesdeuxsalons. co.uk. Main course £16.50–£22.50. Three-course set menu £19.50. AE, DC, MC, V. Lunch, tea & dinner. Tube: Charing Cross. Map p 100.*

★ kids **Maroush V** MARYLEBONE *MIDDLE EASTERN* This branch of a popular London chain, known for its good value, offers a big menu that includes freshly squeezed juices and excellent falafel. Open late. *4 Vere St.* ☎ *020/7493-3030. www.maroush. com. Main course £13–£18. AE, DC, MC, V. Breakfast, lunch & dinner daily. Tube: Bond St. Map p 100.*

★ kids **Mildred's** SOHO *VEGETARIAN* Vegan and vegetarian dishes include stir-fries, tagines, burgers, salads, and juices. Don't skip the

tasty desserts. *45 Lexington St.* ☎ *020/7494-1634. www.mildreds. co.uk. Main course £8–£10. MC, V. Lunch & dinner daily. Tube: Piccadilly. Map p 100.*

★★ kids **Momo** MAYFAIR *MOROCCAN* Decorated in Arabian Nights splendor, this West End success story is a wonderful place for a taste of exotic *tagines* (Moroccan spiced stews) *25 Heddon St.* ☎ *020/7434-4040. www.momoresto.com. Main course £17–£28. AE, DC, MC, V. Lunch & dinner daily. Tube: Piccadilly Circus. Map p 100.*

kids **My Old Dutch Pancake House** CHELSEA *CREPERIE* Stick to the thin pancakes, which are as large as a pizza and topped with whatever you fancy. *221 King's Rd.* ☎ *020/7376-5650. www.myold dutch.com. Main course £8–£11. AE, MC, V. Breakfast, lunch & dinner daily. Tube: Sloane Sq. Map p 98.*

★★★ **Nobu** MAYFAIR *JAPANESE/ FUSION* Famous for its glamor, celebrity customers, and creative sushi. *Metropolitan Hotel, 19 Old Park Lane.* ☎ *020/7447-4747. www. noburestaurants.com. Main course £13–£34. AE, MC, V. Tube: Hyde Park Corner. Map p 100.*

★ kids **Orsini** SOUTH KENSINGTON *ITALIAN* Opposite the V&A, this cafe right out of Naples features great daily specials, perfectly prepared pastas, and super cappuccino. *8a Thurloe Place.* ☎ *020/7581-5553. www.orsiniristorante.com. Main course £8–£15. AE, MC, V. Breakfast, lunch & dinner daily. Tube: S. Kensington. Map p 98.*

★★ **Ottolenghi** ISLINGTON *MEDITERRANEAN* The pick of the various Ottolenghis strewn across town, primarily because this one is a proper restaurant, rather than just a cafe and deli, and it's open all day. The food is healthy and imaginatively prepared. *287 Upper St.* ☎ *020/7288-1454. www.ottolenghi.co.uk. Main course £5.50–£12.50. MC, V. Breakfast, lunch & dinner daily. Tube: Angel or Highbury & Islington. Map p 100.*

★ **Oxo Tower Brasserie** SOUTH-BANK *GLOBAL FUSION* Get the best river views in London while enjoying dishes that combine Mediterranean, French, and Asian ingredients. Dine on the balcony in summer. *Oxo Tower Wharf, Bargehouse St.* ☎ *020/7803-3888. www.harveynichols.com/oxo-tower-london. Main course £18–£32. AE, DC, MC, V. Lunch & dinner daily. Tube: Blackfriars. Map p 100.*

★ kids **The Palm** BELGRAVIA *AMERICAN* Homesick Americans should make a beeline for the Palm, the home of the U.S. chain that serves some of the finest steaks in London (the key lime pie isn't bad either), and has screens showing U.S. sporting events. *1 Point St.* ☎ *020/7201-0710. www.thepalm.com. Main course £17–£49. AE, DC, MC, V. Lunch & dinner daily. Tube: Knightsbridge or Sloane Sq. Map p 100.*

★★ **Poissonnerie de l'Avenue** SOUTH KENSINGTON *FRENCH/SEAFOOD* A very old-school yet very friendly place, with impeccable service, excellent fish, creative French-influenced dishes, and desserts to die for. There's a great two-course set lunch for £22. *82 Sloane Ave.* ☎ *020/7589-2457. www.poissonneriedelavenue.com. Main course £15–£30. AE, DC, MC, V. Lunch & dinner daily. Tube: S. Kensington. Map p 98.*

kids **Porters English Restaurant** COVENT GARDEN *TRADITIONAL BRITISH* Traditional English food, such as steak and kidney pudding, is served in the heart of Theatreland. The comfortable restaurant is family-friendly and lively. Check the website for theatre- or attractions-and-dinner deals. *17 Henrietta St.* ☎ *020/7836-6466. www.porters.uk.com. Main course £12–£18. MC, V. Lunch & dinner daily. Tube: Charing Cross or Covent Garden. Map p 100.*

★★ **The Portrait** SOHO *MODERN BRITISH* There's a gorgeous view over Trafalgar Square, but the food—ranging from chargrilled Scottish sirloin to an elegant afternoon tea—is tasty, too. *The National Portrait Gallery, St. Martin's Lane.* ☎ *020/7312-2490. www.searcys.co.uk/national-portrait-gallery/. Main course £12–£20. AE, DC, MC, V. Breakfast, lunch & afternoon tea daily, dinner Thurs–Fri. Tube: Charing Cross. Map p 100.*

★ kids **The Providores & Tapa Room** MARYLEBONE *GLOBAL* The Tapa Room serves up savory breakfasts; head upstairs to the restaurant for interesting twists on global favorites. *109 Marylebone High St.* ☎ *020/7935-6175. www.theprovidores.co.uk. Main course £10–£20. AE, MC, V. Tapa Room: Breakfast Mon–Fri, brunch & dinner daily. Restaurant: Lunch & dinner daily. Tube: Bond St. Map p 100.*

kids **Rainforest Café** SOHO *AMERICAN* It's not a meal, it's a

The Providores & Tapa Room.

safari loaded with foliage and animatronic animals. Head to this kid-pleasing joint for the atmosphere, and stay for the coconut fried chicken. *20 Shaftesbury Ave.* ☎ *020/7434-3111. www.therainforestcafe. co.uk. Main course £13–£20. AE, DC, MC, V. Lunch & dinner daily. Tube: Piccadilly. Map p 100.*

★★★ kids The Ritz Palm Court

WEST END *ENGLISH TEA* Women, wear your best dress to this very deluxe (and pricey!) tea, served in a Versailles-like setting. Book well in advance. *150 Piccadilly.* ☎ *020/7493-8181. www.theritzlondon.com/tea/. £40 per person. AE, DC, MC, V. Afternoon tea daily. Tube: Green Park. Map p 100.*

★★ kids Roast

SOUTHWARK *BRITISH* Explore Borough market then retreat upstairs for views of St. Paul's. Classic British dishes are made from local, seasonal produce; the contemporary decor adds a twist to the splendor of the historic market architecture. *The Floral Hall, Borough Market, Stoney St.* ☎ *0845/034-7301. www.roast-restaurant.com. Main course £15–£30. AE, MC, V. Breakfast, lunch & dinner daily. Tube: London Bridge. Map p 100.*

★★ kids Royal China Club

MARYLEBONE *CHINESE* This is the real deal for dim sum, with the kind of choice and quality you'd find in Hong Kong. *40–42 Baker St.* ☎ *020/7486-3898. www2.royalchinagroup. biz. Main course £8–£38. AE, MC, V. Lunch & dinner daily. Tube: Baker St. Map p 100.*

★ Rules

COVENT GARDEN *TRADITIONAL ENGLISH* The most traditional Olde English restaurant in London, Rules dates back to 1798, and is a must for Anglophiles and lovers of roast beef and Yorkshire pudding. *35 Maiden Lane.* ☎ *020/7836-5314. www.rules.co.uk. Main course £18–£28. AE, MC, V. Lunch & dinner daily. Tube: Charing Cross. Map p 100.*

★★★ St. John

CLERKENWELL *MODERN BRITISH* Just a hoof's throw from Smithfield Meat Market, this is a carnivore's delight. Founder chef Fergus Henderson uses every part of the animal to create what is known as "nose to tail" eating. Dishes like ox tongue may not be for the squeamish, but they've had food writers raving for years. *26 St. John St.* ☎ *020/3301-8069. www.stjohn restaurant.com. Main course £7–£25. MC, V. Breakfast, lunch*

An afternoon tea at the Ritz.

Tapas Brindisa.

Mon–Fri & Sun, dinner Mon–Sat dinner daily. Tube: Farringdon. Map p 100.

★★ **Scott's** MAYFAIR *FISH/SEA-FOOD* With a giant, shimmering, show-stopping Busby Berkeley arrangement of crustaceans as its centerpiece, this is one of the city's finest fish and seafood restaurants. Menu highlights include octopus carpaccio, smoked haddock with colcannon, and beluga caviar blini with sour cream (a mere £195 for 30g/1 oz). *20 Mount St.* ☎ *020/7495-7309. www.scotts-restaurant. com. Main course £17.50–£32. AE, DC, MC, V. Lunch & dinner daily. Tube: Bond St. Map p 100.*

★★ **Sketch** MAYFAIR *FRENCH/MODERN BRITISH* Sketch is a must-see place, with its beyond-quirky artful decor and variety of eating venues. The Lecture Room and Library, with Michelin-starred chef Pierre Gagnaire, is where the serious gastronomy goes on; but for less money, go for tea or lunch at the Parlour. *9 Conduit St.* ☎ *020/7659-4500. www.sketch.uk.com. Main course £10–£55. AE, DC, MC, V. Lunch & dinner daily. Tube: Oxford Circus. Map p 100.*

★★ **Tamarind** MAYFAIR *INDIAN* Diners ranging from business execs to couples appreciate an imaginative menu that goes beyond the usual curries. *20 Queen St.* ☎ *020/7629-3561. www.tamarindrestaurant. com. Main course £15–£25. AE, DC, MC, V. Lunch Sun–Fri, dinner daily. Tube: Green Park. Map p 100.*

★★ **Tapas Brindisa** BANKSIDE *SPANISH* A top candidate for the title of policy and it can get crowded at weekends, but take a seat at the bar and wait your turn—it'll be worth it. *18 Southwark St.* ☎ *020/7357-8880. www.brindisa.com. Dishes £5–£12.50. AE, DC, MC, V. Lunch & dinner daily, breakfast Sat & Sun. Tube: Southwark. Map p 100.*

kids Texas Embassy Cantina SOHO *TEX MEX* Get knockout margaritas and a Wild West atmosphere in a historic building that once housed the owners of the *Titanic*. *1 Cockspur St.* ☎ *020/7925-0077. www.texasembassy.com. Main course £11–£27. AE, MC, V. Lunch & dinner daily. Tube: Charing Cross. Map p 100.*

kids Vingt Quatre CHELSEA *DINER* The best reason to come to this busy diner is that it's always open, serving brasserie food to jet-lagged

Wagamama.

is tops for reasonably priced Asian food. *4a Streatham St.* ☎ *020/7323-9223. www.wagamama.com. Main course £7–£14. AE, MC, V. Lunch & dinner daily. Tube: Tottenham Court Rd. Map p 100.*

★ kids Whole Foods Market Restaurant KENSINGTON

GLOBAL You'll love the wealth of options and reasonable prices found at the top of the Whole Foods Market building. Excellent takeout and treats to bring back to your hotel room. *63–97 Kensington High St.* ☎ *020/7368-4500. www.wholefoodsmarket.com/stores/kensington/. Main course £4–£15. AE, MC, V. Breakfast, lunch & dinner daily. Tube: Kensington High St. Map p 97.*

★★★ The Wolseley ST. JAMES

ENGLISH This hugely popular restaurant on Piccadilly has a high-ceilinged Art Deco dining room, dishes out celeb sightings, and offers an extensive menu of decent value. And it serves breakfast. *160 Piccadilly.* ☎ *020/7499-6996. www.thewolseley.com. Main course £8–£28. AE, DC, MC, V. Breakfast, lunch & dinner daily. Tube: Green Park. Map p 100.* ●

insomniacs and after-hours club-bers. *325 Fulham Rd.* ☎ *020/7376-7224. www.vingtquatre.co.uk. Main course £9–£14. MC, V. Open 24 hr. Tube: S. Kensington, then bus no. 14. Map p 98.*

kids Wagamama BLOOMSBURY

JAPANESE You sit at large cafeteria-like tables where the noise level is considerable, but this popular chain

Restaurant Deals

Look to the Internet for occasional impressive discounts on London dining. Websites promoting special deals include Last-minute.com and Squaremeal.co.uk. It's also worth subscribing to regular newsletters such as those emailed weekly by Lovefoodlovedrink.co.uk and Travelzoo.com, and signing up to deals websites such as KGB Deals (www.kgbdeals.co.uk/london), LivingSocial (www.livingsocial.com), or Groupon (www.groupon.com). For a top meal at reasonable prices, many destination restaurants offer set-price lunch deals, as well as limited, but top-quality pre- and post-theatre menus; see details in the reviews above. Some London and U.K. newspapers run promotions (usually during January and February) offering lunch or dinner for £5 or £10. Keep an eye on local press.

The Best **Nightlife**

Nightlife Best Bets

Best Dance Club
★★★ Fabric, *77a Charterhouse St.*
(p 123)

Most Diverse Entertainment
★★★ Madame JoJo's, *8–10 Brewer St. (p 123)*

Best Jazz Club
★★★ Ronnie Scott's, *47 Frith St.*
(p 123)

Most Wacky Decor
★ Callooh Callay, *65 Rivington St.*
(p 120)

Best Club to Wear Your Bathing Suit To
★★ Aquarium, *256 Old St. (p 122)*

Most Unpretentious Clubbing
★★ Plastic People, *147–149 Curtain Rd. (p 123)*

Best for Secret Drinking
★★★ The Lamb, *98 Lamb's Conduit St. (p 125)*

Previous page: The Connaught Bar.
Below: The historic Cheshire Cheese.

Best Views
★★★ Vertigo 42, *25 Old Broad St.*
(p 121)

Best Historic Pub
★★★ Ye Olde Cheshire Cheese,
145 Fleet St. (p 127)

Best for Blues
★★ Ain't Nothin' But . . ., *20 Kingly St. (p 119)*

Most Elegant Pub/Bar
★★★ The Audley, *41 Mount St.*
(p 124)

Best Bank Conversion
★★★ The Counting House,
50 Cornhill (p 128)

Best Sports Bar
★ Sports Café, *80 Haymarket*
(p 121)

Best Gay Venue
★★ Heaven, *Villiers St. (p 123)*

Best Cocktail Lounge
★★ Blue Bar, *Berkeley Hotel, Wilton Place (p 120)*

Best Hotel Bar
★★★ The Connaught Bar,
Connaught Hotel, Carlos Place
(p 120)

Best Cocktails
★★ BBar, *43 Buckingham Palace Rd.*
(p 119)

Most Seductive
★★★ Beduin, *57–59 Charterhouse St. (p 120)*

Most Impressive Washrooms
★★ Sketch, *9 Conduit St. (p 124)*

Best People-Watching
Chinawhite, *4 Winsley St. (p 122)*

Best Overall Venue
★★★ Proud Bar, *Stables Market, Chalk Farm Rd. (p 121)*

Notting Hill Nightlife

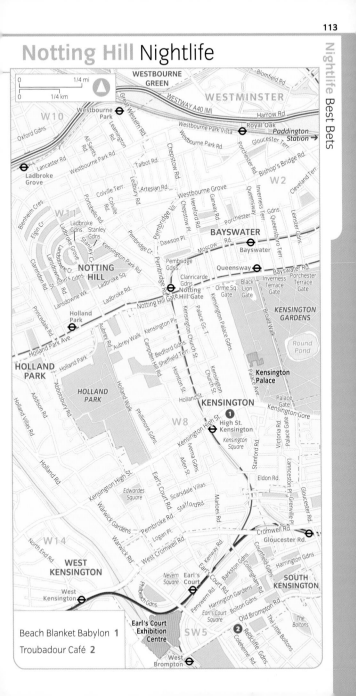

Beach Blanket Babylon **1**

Troubadour Café **2**

West End Nightlife

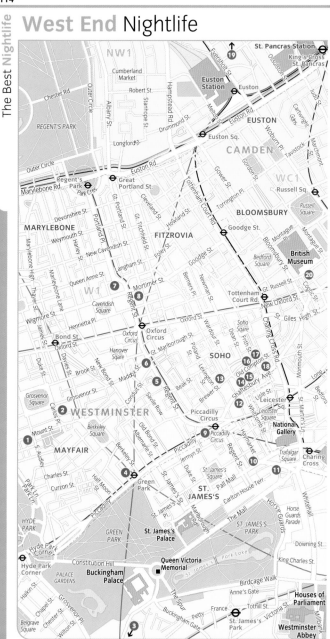

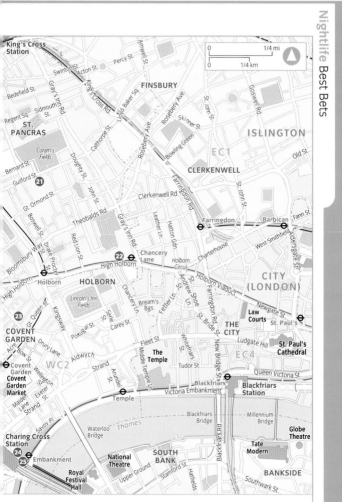

Admiral Duncan 16
Ain't Nothin' But ... 5
Albannach 11
Artesian 7
The Audley 1
Bar Rumba 12
BBar 3
Chinawhite 9
Cittie of York 22

Coach & Horses 18
The Connaught
  Bar 2
Gordon's 25
Green Carnation 15
Guanabara 23
Heaven 24
The Lamb 21
Madame JoJo's 13

Museum Tavern 20
Proud Bar 19
The Rivoli Bar 4
Ronnie Scott's 17
Sketch 6
The Social 8
Sports Café 10
Waxy
  O'Connors 14

Kensington Nightlife

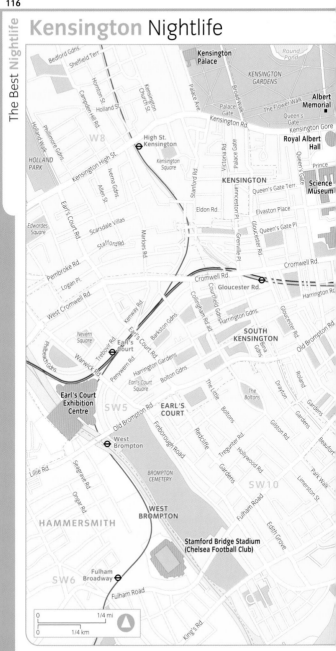

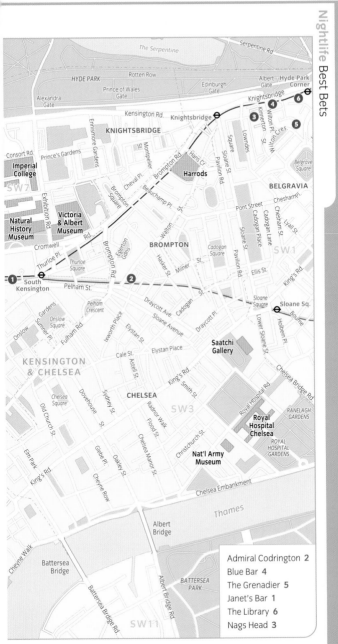

Admiral Codrington 2
Blue Bar 4
The Grenadier 5
Janet's Bar 1
The Library 6
Nags Head 3

Nightlife in The City

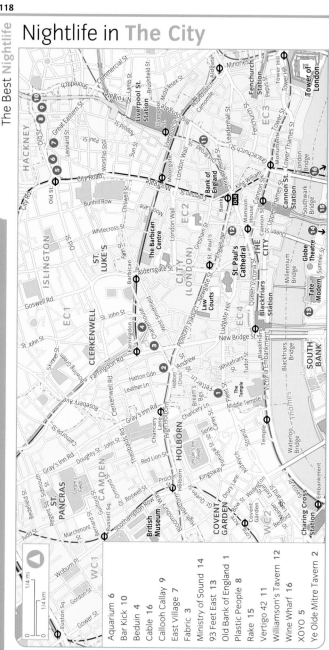

Aquarium 6
Bar Kick 10
Beduin 4
Cable 16
Callooh Callay 9
East Village 7
Fabric 3
Ministry of Sound 14
93 Feet East 13
Old Bank of England 1
Plastic People 8
Rake 15
Vertigo 42 11
Williamson's Tavern 12
Wine Wharf 16
XOYO 5
Ye Olde Mitre Tavern 2

London Nightlife A to Z

Bars

★★ Ain't Nothin' But . . . SOHO A tiny blues joint plucked straight from the bayou; it may not be Bourbon Street, but there's good jambalaya and live blues every night of the week. *20 Kingly St.* ☎ *020/7287-0514. www.aintnothinbut.co.uk. Tube: Piccadilly Circus. Map p 114.*

★ Albannach WESTMINSTER Where most bars aim to serve as wide a range of drinks as possible, the Albannach places most of its emphasis on just one—Scotch whisky—offering a huge number, ranging from a couple of quid for a shot to over £750. The bar is Scottish themed—expect kilted staff—and there's also an attached restaurant. *66 Trafalgar Sq.* ☎ *020/7930-0066. www.albannach.co.uk. Tube: Charing Cross. Map p 114.*

★★ Artesian MARYLEBONE Terribly swanky and expensive, Artesian has some of the most opulent decor this side of royalty; the interior is a riot of silver-leaf mirrors and huge chandeliers. Take plenty of money and make your drinks last—the special, denser, longer-lasting ice cubes will help. *Langham Hotel, 1c Portland Pl.* ☎ *020/7636-1000. www.artesian-bar. co.uk. Tube: Oxford Circus. Map p 114.*

★ Bar Kick SHOREDITCH Every bar needs to stand out from the crowd. Bar Kick's theme is, appropriately enough, kicking things. The interior is filled with table football and there are TVs showing live matches. Don't go expecting a rowdy pub, however. It's in Shoreditch, so the regulars are far too cool to get that excited. *127 Shoreditch High St.* ☎ *020/7739-8700. www.cafekick.co.uk. Tube: Shoreditch High St. Map p 118.*

★★ BBar VICTORIA This trendy bar with an African-inspired decor serves more than 60 cocktails. There's a vast wine cellar and a fusion menu of appetizing noshes. *43 Buckingham Palace Rd.* ☎ *020/ 7958-7000. www.bbarlondon.com. Tube: Victoria. Map p 114.*

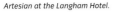

Artesian at the Langham Hotel.

Beach Blanket Babylon NOTTING HILL   Truly wacko decor (a fireplace shaped like a tiger's mouth, a gangplank, and other kitschy excesses) will bring a smile to your lips that the often lousy service won't entirely wipe off. *45 Ledbury Rd.* 📞 *020/7229-2907. www.beachblanket.co.uk. Tube: Notting Hill Gate. Map p 113.*

★★★ **Beduin** FARRINGDON   It's the height of sophistication, thanks to a stylish Moroccan souk decor (red sofas, silver tables, and so on) spread out over three floors. *57–59 Charterhouse St.* 📞 *020/7336-6484. www.beduin-london.co.uk. Tube: Farringdon. Map p 118.*

★★ **Blue Bar** KNIGHTSBRIDGE   In the lovely Berkeley Hotel, this tiny (50-person) and, yes, blue (Luyten's blue, to be exact) bar serves more than 50 varieties of whisky and tapas-type snacks to a very upscale crowd. *Wilton Place.* 📞 *020/7235-6000. www.the-berkeley.co.uk. Tube: Hyde Park Corner. Map p 116.*

★ **Calloon Callay** SHOREDITCH   It's very Shoreditch, with plenty of wacky touches—gramophone punch bowls, a wardrobe linking the two bars, crazy mismatched decor—but also plenty of fun, attracting a young, hip crowd. The name is derived from *Jabberwocky*, the Lewis Carroll nonsense poem, in case you were wondering. *65 Rivington St.* 📞 *020/7739-4781. www.calloohcallaybar.com. Tube: Hoxton or Old St. Map p 118.*

★★★ **The Connaught Bar** MAYFAIR   The Connaught Bar is where guests at this most traditional, old-style hotel go to let off a little steam. It's as sparkling and fun as the hotel is quiet and reserved. *Carlos Place.* 📞 *020/7499-7070. www.the-connaught.co.uk. Tube: Bond St. Map p 114.*

★★ **Gordon's** COVENT GARDEN   Gordon's first began serving drinks back in 1890, and if either the decor or the wine list has changed since then it's news to us. This gloomy, subterranean place is an absolute institution. Other bars may be swankier, but few can compete for atmosphere. *47 Villiers St.* 📞 *020/7940-1408. www.gordonswinebar.com. Tube: Embankment. Map p 114.*

★ **Green Carnation** SOHO   Inspired by Oscar Wilde, this

Blue Bar at the Berkeley Hotel.

highbrow salon is lavish and classy. Upstairs is relaxed, downstairs more boisterous. Try the raspberry *caipiroska*, with vodka, fresh lime, and raspberries. *5 Greek St.* 020/8123-4267. *www.greencarnationsoho. co.uk. Tube: Tottenham Court Rd. Map p 114.*

★★ **Guanabara** HOLBORN Chic Latin bar where Brazilian artists play Latin cool, funk, samba, and Brazilian jazz in a spacious modern interior. Try one of the exotic, cutting-edge cocktails. You won't be able to stand still. *Parker St., corner of Drury Lane.* 020/7242-8600. *www.guanabara. co.uk. Tube: Holborn. Map p 114.*

★ **Janet's Bar** SOUTH KENSINGTON Owned by an expat, ex-lawyer Yankee (the eponymous Janet), this is a bar with attitude—it's very kitsch and a lot of fun. There's live music on Thursday, Friday, and Saturday nights. *30 Old Brompton Rd.* 020/7581-3160. *Tube: S. Kensington. Map p 116.*

★★ **The Library** KNIGHTSBRIDGE Business execs on expense accounts sip cocktails and cognac at this sophisticated bar in the Lanesborough hotel. A roaring fire and tinkling piano complete the picture. *1 Lanesborough Place.* 020/7259-5599. *www.lanesborough.com. Tube: Hyde Park Corner. Map p 116.*

★ **93 Feet East** SHOREDITCH DJs spin funk, hip-hop, disco, rock, and indie in a large space that includes a main bar with a stage for live music, an intimate gallery bar with bench seating, and a pink bar with comfy sofas. *150 Brick Lane.* 020/7770-6006. *www.93feeteast.co.uk. Tube: Aldgate E. Map p 118.*

★★★ **Proud Bar** CAMDEN Situated in a 200-year-old horse hospital, this immense bar, photo gallery, and music venue is achingly hip and visually stunning. The gig room

hosts big-name stars, while the huge outdoor terrace is perfect in summer. *Stables Market, Chalk Farm Rd.* 020/7424-3867. *www.proud camden.com. Tube: Chalk Farm. Map p 114.*

★★ **Rake** BANKSIDE Just around the corner from Borough Market, this absolutely tiny bar serves, by way of contrast, one of the capital's widest selections of independent beers. There are more than 160, way more than there ever are people. There's also a small garden. *14 Winchester Walk.* 020/7407-0557. *Tube: London Bridge. Map p 118.*

★★★ **The Rivoli Bar** WEST END The Ritz Hotel's restored Art Deco bar offers all the atmosphere you would expect from this bastion of over-the-top swank, as well as a varied drinks menu. A strict dress code keeps the young at bay. *150 Piccadilly.* 020/7493-8181. *www.theritz london.com/rivoliBar/. Tube: Green Park. Map p 114.*

★ **Sports Café** WEST END When you need your sports fix, this is the place: 120 TVs, seven pool tables, three bars, a dance floor, and four giant screens of games, games, and more games. *80 Haymarket.* 020/7839-8300. *www.thesportscafe.net. Tube: Piccadilly Circus. Map p 114.*

★★ **Troubadour Café** EARL'S COURT Yes, it's a restaurant, but it's also a pub, a wine bar, and bohemian hangout. There are poetry readings, live music, and singer-songwriter nights in the warren of small rooms. *265 Old Brompton Rd.* 020/7370-1434. *www.troubadour. co.uk. Tube: Earl's Court. Map p 113.*

★★★ **Vertigo 42** THE CITY On the 42nd floor of the City's second-tallest skyscraper, this champagne bar is the highest in England and features splendid (and rare for London) views. It's the perfect place to sip a cocktail at sunset. *Tower 42, 25 Old Broad St.* ☎ *020/7877-7842.* www. *vertigo42.co.uk.* Tube: Liverpool St. Map p 118.

Waxy O'Connors WEST END

This roaring Irish bar features mad Gaelic music, tipsy crowds, and a shameless sort of tourist appeal. The weird decor improves with each drink—you'll love the indoor tree. *14–16 Rupert St.* ☎ *020/7287-0255.* www.waxyoconnors.co.uk. Tube: Leicester Sq. Map p 114.

★ Wine Wharf BANKSIDE An

off-shoot of the wine museum Vinopolis, Wine Wharf is to wines what Rake (above) is to beer, with some 250 vintages available, many by the glass. As you make your way through the list you can take advantage of the sofas helpfully scattered around the venue. A range of bar snacks helps soak up the excess alcohol. *Stoney St.* ☎ *020/7940-8335.* www.winewharf.co.uk. Tube: London Bridge. Map p 118.

Dance Clubs & Live Music
★★ Aquarium EAST END This crazy nightclub offers you the chance to shed your clothes and jump in a pool with strangers. Germaphobes may want to stick to the fully clothed drinking and dancing. *256 Old St.* ☎ *020/7253-3558.* www. *clubaquarium.co.uk.* £8–£38 cover. Tube: Old St. Map p 118.

★★ Bar Rumba SOHO An inti-

mate basement venue with mood lighting and leather couches. The music is a mix of commercial dance, R&B, and party classics, and there are social evenings and comedy nights. *36 Shaftesbury Ave.* ☎ *020/7287-6933.* www.barrumba.co.uk. £5–£12 cover after 9pm. Tube: Leicester Sq. Map p 114.

★ Cable BANKSIDE A shimmy or

two from London Bridge, the subterranean confines of one of London's top clubs contain several bars and dance areas. The coolest spot is on the mezzanine, where you can look down on the heaving hordes below. *33a Bermondsey St.* ☎ *020/7403-7730.* www.cable-london.com. Tube: London Br. Map p 11.

Chinawhite WEST END Now in

new Fitzrovia premises, the original celebs and aristos party venue is still pulling in the punters with its heady mix of oriental decor, high-price drinks, and whiff of privilege. *4 Winsley St.* ☎ *020/790-0580.* www. *chinawhite.com.* £15–£20 cover. Tube: Oxford Circus. Map p 114.

The Connaught Bar.

Ronnie Scott's.

★ **East Village** EAST END   The upstairs Villain bar is pretty fancy, with its leather car seats and expensive lighting (happy hour 5–8pm Tues–Fri), but the basement dance space is about as utilitarian as you can get, consisting of a DJ booth, a dance floor and a single sofa (you'll have to take it in turns recuperating). Music is overwhelmingly house oriented. *89 Gt. Eastern St.* ☎ *020/7739-5173. www.eastvillageclub.co.uk. Tube: Old St. Map p 118.*

★★★ **Fabric** EAST END   A favorite with London's committed weekend partygoers and hot-off-the-press vinyl lovers. Dance till 5am to the drum & bass, electro, and techno beats on the "bodysonic" dance floor, where you can feel the music's vibrations through your feet. *77a Charterhouse St.* ☎ *020/7336-8898. www.fabriclondon.com. Tube: Farringdon. Map p 118.*

★★ **Heaven** COVENT GARDEN Now home to G-A-Y, following the demolition of the Astoria, this landmark venue, with more than 25 years of partying under its belt, is growing old disgracefully. *Under the Arches, Villiers St.* ☎ *020/7930-2020. www.heaven-london.com. £6–£15 cover. Tube: Embankment. Map p 114.*

★★★ **Madame JoJo's** SOHO This unpretentiously cool spot has a well-earned reputation as one of Soho's most fun clubs, with decent drink prices and a good dance floor. The offerings range from club nights, burlesque, and comedy to Saturday-night drag queens. *8–10 Brewer St.* ☎ *020/7734-3040. www.madamejojos.com. £4–£52.50 cover. Tube: Piccadilly. Map p 114.*

★★★ **Ministry of Sound** ELE-PHANT & CASTLE   This legendary venue has seen competitors come and go over its 20-year history, but it's still going strong with four bars, three huge dance floors, and a hefty sound system playing techno, hip-hop, funk, house, and garage. E-mail ahead to get on the guest list. *103 Gaunt St.* ☎ *020/7378-6562. www.ministryofsound.com. £13–£20 cover. Tube: Elephant & Castle. Map p 118.*

★★ **Plastic People** EAST END   For true music aficionados, the decidedly unpretentious P.P. offers live jazz, Latin, techno, soul, hip-hop, house, and funk. Ironically named, it attracts a casual, jovial crowd. *147–149 Curtain Rd.* ☎ *020/7739-6471. www.plasticpeople.co.uk. £7–£15 cover. Tube: Old St. Map p 118.*

★★★ **Ronnie Scott's** SOHO Open since 1959, this granddaddy of London's jazz clubs fully deserves its legendary reputation. The best jazz musicians in the world play this classy but relaxed venue every night. *47 Frith St. ☎ 020/7439-0747. www. ronniescotts.co.uk. £20–£25 cover. Tube: Leicester Sq. Map p 114.*

★★ Sketch MAYFAIR Glitzy, glam, and riotously decorated, Sketch attracts celeb visitors and well-heeled regulars by successfully combining food, music, drinking, and art. *9 Conduit St. ☎ 020/7659-4500. www.sketch.uk.com. Tube: Oxford Circus. Map p 114.*

★★ The Social FITZROVIA Civilized and unpretentious, this club hosts a casual, eclectic crowd, including the occasional celeb. It's tiny, but there's an evening jukebox, late-night DJs, and fun food. *5 Little Portland St. ☎ 020/7636-4992. www.thesocial. com. Tube: Oxford Circus. Map p 114.*

★ XOYO EAST END A fine addition to Shoreditch's ever-expanding collection of clubs, this former print works is a place for dancing, not chilling (there are no seats), laying on a mixture of DJ sets and live music. Up to 800 revelers can gyrate away inside its cavernous industrial confines. *32–37 Cowper St. ☎ 020/7490-1198. www.xoyo.co.uk. £5–£13.50 cover. Tube: Old St. Map p 118.*

Pubs

★ Admiral Codrington CHELSEA This pub has modern British cuisine, a well-heeled crowd, and a nice atmosphere, made all the better on summer days by the retractable glass roof. Outdoor tables handle overflow on warm evenings. *17 Mossop St. ☎ 020/7581-0005. Tube: S. Kensington. Map p 116.*

★ Admiral Duncan SOHO This popular gay bar offers bargain shots, cocktails, and a good selection of wines. Gay or straight, it's a mellow and friendly place to drink.

The Lamb.

54 Old Compton St. ☎ 020/7437-5300. Tube: Leicester Sq. Map p 114.

★★★ The Audley MAYFAIR This is one of London's more beautiful old-school pubs, evocative of a Victorian-era gentlemen's club (it was built in the 1880s). Slip into a booth beneath the original chandeliers and sample the traditional English grub. *41 Mount St. ☎ 020/7499-1843. Tube: Green Park. Map p 114.*

★ Cittie of York BLOOMSBURY There's been a pub on this site since 1430, and though the current building dates back "only" to the 1890s there's still a (faux) old-world vibe, and (real) ale. Check out the church-like interior and its immense wine vats. Closed Sunday. *22 High Holborn. ☎ 020/7242-7670. Tube: Chancery Lane. Map p 114.*

★★ Coach & Horses SOHO Perhaps the ultimate, pared-down, no-nonsense English pub, that inspired Keith Waterhouse's play *Jeffrey Bernard Is Unwell.* It has bags of character and attracts an interesting crowd. *29 Greek St. ☎ 020/7437-5920. Tube: Oxford Circus. Map p 114.*

★★ The Grenadier BELGRAVIA This charming pub, tucked away in a secluded mews, is best known for its Bloody Marys, resident ghost, and military past (the Duke of Wellington's soldiers used it as their mess hall). *18 Wilton Row.* ☎ *020/7235-3074. Tube: Knightsbridge. Map p 116.*

★★★ **The Lamb** BLOOMSBURY You'll find one of the city's few remaining "snob screens"—used to protect drinkers from prying eyes—at this Victorian pub. Those who've enjoyed the anonymity here include the Bloomsbury Group and Charles Dickens. *98 Lamb's Conduit St.* ☎ *020/7405-0713. Tube: Russell Sq. Map p 114.*

★ **Museum Tavern** BLOOMSBURY This early 18th-century pub, the former Dog & Duck, changed its name when the British Museum was built across the street in the 1760s. The old-style decor remains intact. *49 Great Russell St.* ☎ *020/7242-8987. Tube: Russell Sq. Map p 114.*

★★ **Nags Head** BELGRAVIA This rarity, an independently owned pub, was built in the early 19th century for the posh area's workers. A "no phones" rule attempts to keep the

21st century from intruding. *53 Kinnerton St.* ☎ *020/7235-1135. Tube: Knightsbridge. Map p 116.*

★ **Old Bank of England** THE CITY This unusual pub is housed in a converted former bank that has retained all the majesty of a palace of finance, with a huge interior and wonderful murals. It's a City hangout, so it's closed on weekends. *194 Fleet St.* ☎ *020/7430-2255. Tube: Temple. Map p 118.*

★★ **Williamson's Tavern** EAST END With a history that goes back to Londinium (there are excavated Roman tiles in the fireplace), this pub lies in an alley fronted by gates that were gifts of William III and Mary II. *1 Groveland Court.* ☎ *020/7248-6280. Tube: Mansion House. Map p 118.*

★★★ **Ye Olde Mitre Tavern** EAST END Good service, beamed ceilings, and the stump of a tree Queen Elizabeth I reportedly frolicked under make this historic treasure a must-see. It's hard to find, but do try. *Ely Court, off Ely Place.* ☎ *020/7405-4751. Tube: Chancery Lane. Map p 118.*

Ye Olde Mitre Tavern.

London **Pub Crawl**

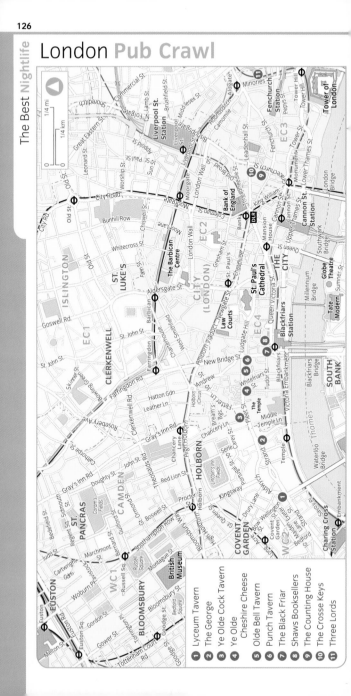

1 Lyceum Tavern
2 The George
3 Ye Olde Cock Tavern
4 Ye Olde
   Cheshire Cheese
5 Olde Bell Tavern
6 Punch Tavern
7 The Black Friar
8 Shaws Booksellers
9 The Counting House
10 The Crosse Keys
11 Three Lords

If London is, as has often been claimed, less a single, cohesive city than a collection of villages, then its pubs are the hearts of those villages. A local is a place to wind down after work, hang out with friends at the weekend, and, of course, get rip-roaring drunk. This evening jaunt explores some of the City's best and then heads east. START: **Temple Tube Station.**

1 ★ Lyceum Tavern. The two floors of this Strand stalwart have very different personalities. Downstairs it's dark and snug, the space divided into separate booths with tables and benches. The upstairs area, where food is served, is open plan with a large window giving views of the comings and goings on Waterloo Bridge. It's run by Samuel Smith's Brewery, so prices are reasonable. *354 Strand.* ☎ *020/7836-7155. Map p 126.*

2 ★ The George. Just across from the Royal Courts of Justice, this was a coffeehouse when it opened in 1723 and was frequented by scribblers Horace Walpole, Oliver Goldsmith, and the ubiquitous Dr. Samuel Johnson. A pub since Victorian times, it still has beautiful (if faux) medieval timbering and stained glass. *213 Strand.* ☎ *020/7353-9638. Map p 126.*

3 Ye Olde Cock Tavern. The main reason to come to this pub is its architecture: The cockerel was supposedly made by master carver Grinling Gibbons, and much of the building survived the Great Fire of London and dates back to the 16th century. It was a favorite of Dickens, Samuel Pepys, and Alfred Lord Tennyson (who mentioned it in one of his poems, a copy of which hangs near the entrance). Check out the occasional quiz night. *22 Fleet St.* ☎ *020/7353-8570. Map p 126.*

4 ★★★ Ye Olde Cheshire Cheese. This wonderfully atmospheric, labyrinthine old pub was rebuilt right after the fire of 1666 and hasn't changed much since. Dr. Samuel Johnson lived around the corner, and other literary ghosts haunt the place. It's also operated by the Samuel Smith's Brewery, whose pints are amongst the cheapest in the capital. *Wine Office Court, 145 Fleet St.* ☎ *020/7353-6170. Map p 126.*

5 ★★ Olde Bell Tavern. This cozy and authentic pub was built in the 1670s for workmen constructing St. Bride's (the "wedding cake" church designed by Wren in 1670), and maintains an old-world ambience with its leaded windows and wainscoted walls. The pub's

Ye Old Cheshire Cheese.

laidback, genial atmosphere makes it a good spot for a pint—it serves half a dozen hand-pulled ales. Closed weekends. *95 Fleet St.* ☎ *020/7583-0216. Map p 126.*

6 ★★ **Punch Tavern.** Bearing the scars of an ownership feud that divided the premises in two, this Victorian pub was the place where *Punch* was founded in 1841; look for artifacts from that magazine (as well as *Punch & Judy*-themed memorabilia) on the walls. The bright interior features some beautifully etched mirrors and art nouveau chandeliers. Closed Sunday. *99 Fleet St.* ☎ *020/7353-6658. Map p 126.*

7 ★★★ **The Black Friar.** The amazingly detailed interior of this wedge-shaped Arts & Crafts pub is a feast for the eye. The magnificently carved friezes of monks remind you that the pub was built on the site of a 13th-century Dominican monastery, and under the vaulted ceiling you'll find such inscribed thoughts as WISDOM IS RARE. It's a popular after-work watering hole for the City's business set. *174 Queen Victoria St.* ☎ *020/7236-5474. Map p 126.*

8 ★ **Shaws Booksellers.** This is as much a wine bar and a restaurant as it is a pub, though it performs each role well. It's set in a restored paper merchant's warehouse, with an elegant curved glass frontage. Expect upmarket be-suited clientele

and a long wine list. *31–34 St. Andrew's Hill. Queen Victoria St.* ☎ *020/7489-7999. Map p 126.*

9 ★★★ **The Counting House.** A former bank, this must-see pub has a wonderfully opulent interior with a glass dome, a balcony (great for people-watching), extravagant chandeliers, gilded mirrors, and marbled walls. Prices are a little steep. *50 Cornhill* ☎ *020/7283-7123. Map p 126.*

10 ★★ **The Crosse Keys.** Very grand, this former bank is now an elegant pub with three separate eating rooms, a courtyard, high ceilings, wonderful wall carvings, and glass domes. It's almost too stately to be a pub. Part of the Wetherspoon chain, the food and drink are very reasonably priced for the area. Closed Sunday. *9 Gracechurch St.* ☎ *020/7623-4824. Map p 126.*

11 **Three Lords.** First founded in the 18th century and named after three Scottish aristocrats who were executed just down the road on Tower Hill for their part in the failed 1745 Jacobite Rebellion, the current version of the pub dates back only to the 1980s. It's still a very traditional affair, however, with a dark-wood interior and a boisterous, cheery atmosphere, particularly toward the end of the week. *30–33 Minories.* ☎ *020/7481-4249. Map p 126.* ●

8 The Best Arts & Entertainment

Arts & Entertainment Best Bets

Best for a **Laugh**
★★★ The Comedy Store, *1a Oxendon St. (p 135)*

Best for **Opera**
★★★ Royal Opera House, *Covent Garden (p 134)*

Best **Baroque Concerts**
★ St. Martin-in-the-Fields Evening Candlelight Concerts, *Trafalgar Sq. (p 135)*

Best **Restored Venue**
★★★ Royal Albert Hall, *Kensington Gore (p 134)*

Most **Comfortable Movie Theatre Seats**
★★ The Electric Cinema, *191 Portobello Rd. (p 136)*

Best for a **Cheap Movie Date**
★★ Prince Charles Cinema, *7 Leicester Place (p 136)*

Most **Old-Fashioned Cinema**
★★ Coronet Cinema, *Notting Hill Gate (p 136)*

Best **Free Live-Music Performances**
★★ LSO St. Luke's, *161 Old St. (p 134)*

Best for **Independent Films**
★ Curzon Mayfair, *38 Curzon St. (p 136)*

Best **Pop Concert Venue**
★★ O2 Arena, *Peninsula Sq. (p 134)*

Best **Outdoor Performances**
★★ Open Air Theatre, *Inner Circle, Regent's Park (p 137)*

Best **Ballet**
★★★ Sadler's Wells, *Rosebery Ave. (p 136)*

Best **Symphony**
★★★ London Symphony Orchestra at the Barbican Centre, *Silk St. (p 134)*

Best **Modern Dance**
★★ The Place, *17 Duke's Rd. (p 135)*

Best **New Playwrights**
★★ Royal Court Theatre, *Sloane Sq. (p 137)*

Best **Shakespeare**
★★★ Shakespeare's Globe Theatre, *21 New Globe Walk (p 137)*

Best **Theatrical Repertory Company**
★★★ Royal National Theatre, *South Bank (p 137)*

Longest-**Running Musical**
★★ Les Misérables, *Queen's Theatre, Shaftesbury Ave. (p 138)*

Dance at Sadler's Wells.

West End **Theatres**

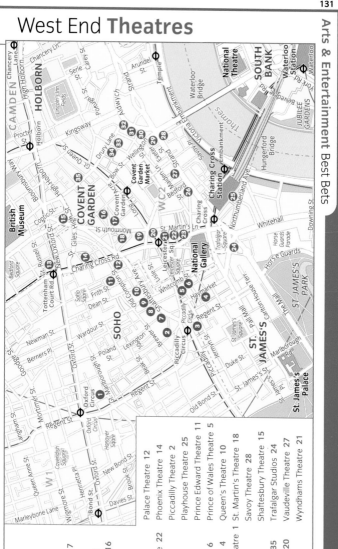

London **Arts & Entertainment**

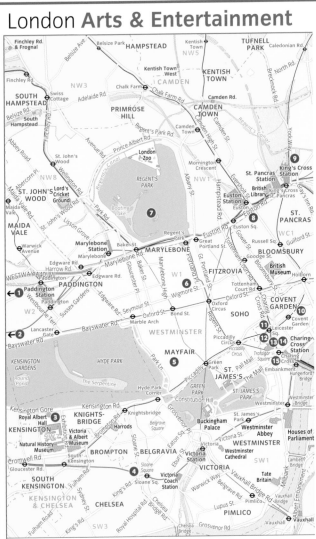

Amused Moose Soho **11**

Barbican Centre **22**

Comedy Café **23**

The Comedy Store **13**

Coronet Cinema **2**

Curzon Mayfair **5**

The Electric Cinema **1**

King's Place **9**

London Coliseum **15**

LSO St. Luke's **21**

The Old Vic **18**

Open Air Theatre **7**

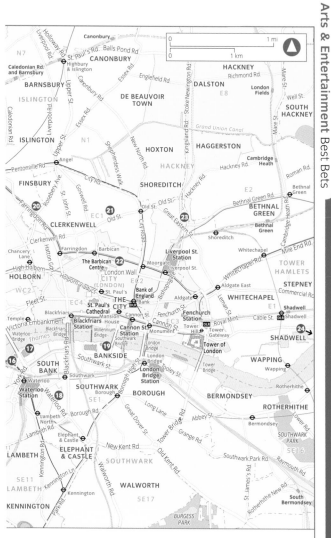

O2 Arena **24**

The Place **8**

Prince Charles Cinema **12**

Royal Albert Hall **3**

Royal Court Theatre **4**

Royal Festival Hall **16**

Royal National Theatre **17**

Royal Opera House **10**

Sadler's Wells **20**

St. Martin-in-the-Fields **14**

Shakespeare's Globe Theatre **19**

Wigmore Hall **6**

London A&E A to Z

Classical, Opera & Popular Music

★★★ **Barbican Centre** THE CITY
A gargantuan 1980s' venue, the Barbican's acoustics make it the best place for hearing music in the U.K. It's home to the first-class **London Symphony Orchestra,** and puts on regular free concerts in its foyer. Performances of dance and theatre are also staged. *Silk St.* ☎ *020/7638-8891. www.barbican.org.uk. Tickets £10–£30. Tube: Barbican. Map p 132.*

★ **King's Place** KING'S CROSS
London's latest major concert venue opened a couple of years back in a giant new development at King's Cross. It's the home of the **London Sinfonietta** and its acoustics are notoriously precise—don't be rustling any candy wrappers unless you want a row full of dirty looks. There are jazz and dance performances too. *90 York Way.* ☎ *020/7520-1490. www.kingsplace.co.uk. Tickets £2.50–£34.50. Tube: King's Cross. Map p 132.*

★★ **London Coliseum** WEST END
Converted into an opera house in 1968, London's largest theatre is home to the **English National Opera.** Productions range from Gilbert and Sullivan to more challenging modern fare; most are staged in English. *St. Martin's Lane.* ☎ *020/7836-0111. www.eno.org. Tickets £15–£91. Tube: Charing Cross. Map p 132.*

★★ **LSO St. Luke's** OLD STREET
Designed by Hawksmoor, this deconsecrated church provides an alternative 370-seat venue for the **London Symphony Orchestra** (when it's not at the Barbican). It puts on cheap lunchtime concerts and it is occasionally possible to watch the orchestra practice for free. *161 Old St.* ☎ *020/7588-1116.*

http://lso.co.uk. Tickets free–£25. Tube: Old St. Map p 132.

★★ **O2 Arena** GREENWICH The massive interior of the previously underused Millennium Dome is now the most modern entertainment venue in England. Alongside the 20,000-seat arena is a smaller concert hall, the Indigo2, with good acoustics and comfortable seats. *Peninsula Sq.* ☎ *0844/856-0202. www.theo2.co.uk. Tickets £10–£150. Tube: N. Greenwich. Map 132.*

★★★ **Royal Albert Hall** KENSINGTON This splendid Victorian pleasure palace is best known as the home of the city's annual **Henry Wood Promenade Concerts (the Proms)** in summer, when you'll hear orchestral classics and chamber music. Pop, rock, and jazz are offered at other times. *Kensington Gore.* ☎ *0845/401-5045. www.royalalberthall.com. Tickets £4.25–£80. Tube: High St. Kensington. Map p 132.*

★★★ **Royal Festival Hall** SOUTH BANK More than 150,000 hours of music have been performed at this acoustically exceptional complex since it opened in 1951. The hall's many free and low-priced concerts make it a great bet for those on a budget. *Belvedere Rd.* ☎ *0844/875-0073. www.southbankcentre.co.uk. Tickets £9–£55. Tube: Waterloo. Map p 132.*

★★★ **Royal Opera House** COVENT GARDEN The magnificent theatre occupies one corner of Covent Garden. Operas are sung in the original language. Make an evening of it with dinner in the Balconies restaurant. *Covent Garden.* ☎ *020/7304-4000. www.royaloperahouse.org. Tickets £6–£285. Tube: Covent Garden. Map p 132.*

Royal Albert Hall.

★ **St. Martin-in-the-Fields** WEST END Follow (allegedly) in Mozart's footsteps, and attend a concert at this atmospheric church. Admission to its popular lunchtime concerts (Mon, Tues, and Fri at 1pm) is by suggested donation (£3.50). Jazz and classical make up the bulk of the evening repertoire. *Trafalgar Sq. ☎ 020/7766-1100. www.stmartin-in-the-fields.org. Tickets £5.50–£24. Tube: Charing Cross. Map p 132.*

★★ **Wigmore Hall** MARYLEBONE Bechstein Pianos built this grand Renaissance-style recital hall—one of the world's finest—in 1901. The greatest names in classical music have taken advantage of this venue's fabulous acoustics. *36 Wigmore St. ☎ 020/7935-2141. www.wigmore-hall.org.uk. Tickets £10–£35. Tube: Bond St. Map p 132.*

Comedy
★ **Amused Moose Soho** SOHO Situated above a popular gay bar, this Thursday-through-Saturday comedy club has showcased such epic knee-slappers as Eddie Izzard. *Moonlighting, 17 Greek St. ☎ 020/7287-3727. www.amusedmoose. com. Tickets £8. Tube: Leicester Sq. Map p 132.*

★★ **Comedy Café** EAST END Crowded tables and exposed brick walls provide an appropriate setting for raw comedy and plenty of heckling. Wednesday is "open mic" night, and it's free. Closed Sunday to Tuesday. *68 Rivington St. ☎ 020/7739-5706. www.comedycafe.co.uk. Tickets £10–£16. Tube: Old St. Map p 132.*

★★★ **The Comedy Store** PICCADILLY CIRCUS The club that, in a previous incarnation, launched the alternative comedy boom of the early 1980s, this is still very much the venue at which up-and-coming comics aspire to perform. It attracts a mixture of both newbies and big names. *1a Oxendon St. ☎ 0844/871-7699. www.thecomedystore. co.uk. Tickets free–£20. Tube: Piccadilly Circus. Map p 132.*

Dance
★★ **The Place** BLOOMSBURY Dedicated to both the teaching and the performing of dance, this small venue is the place in London to see contemporary new artists and startling modern dance. *17 Duke's Rd. ☎ 020/7121-1100. www.theplace.org.uk. Tickets £3–£17. Tube: Euston. Map p 132.*

The Curzon Mayfair cinema.

★★★ Royal Opera House

COVENT GARDEN   The brilliantly restored 19th-century ROH houses the even more brilliant **Royal Ballet,** a company on a par with the world's best. You can catch any number of classics, such as *Swan Lake, Giselle,* or *Sleeping Beauty,* but you'll pay for the privilege. *See p 132.*

★★★ Sadler's Wells ISLINGTON

The best dance troupes in the world—from cutting edge to classical—are delighted to perform at this chic theatre, where they are assured of modern facilities and an appreciative audience. *Rosebery Ave.* ☎ *0844/412-4300. www.sadlers wells.com. Tickets £10–£38. Tube: Angel. Map p 132.*

Movies

★★ Coronet Cinema NOTTING

HILL   London's oldest-operating (and reputedly haunted) movie theatre first opened in 1923, and its lovely balcony has been seating popcorn throwers ever since. Tickets are half-price on Tuesday. *Notting Hill Gate.* ☎ *020/7727-6705. www.coronetcinema.co.uk. Tickets*

£4.50–£7. *Tube: Notting Hill Gate. Map p 132.*

★ Curzon Mayfair MAYFAIR

This historic art-house theatre (it dates back to 1934) is famous for its world cinema screenings. *38 Curzon St.* ☎ *020/7495-0500. www.curzon cinemas.com. Tickets £7–£12.50. Tube: Green Park. Map p 132.*

★★ kids The Electric Cinema

NOTTING HILL   Couches and leather seats, cocktails and yummy treats, Sunday double features, and weekly mother-and-baby screenings make this art house a destination theatre. Mainstream and independent films are shown. *191 Portobello Rd.* ☎ *020/7908-9696. www.electric cinema.co.uk. Tickets £14.50–£18. Tube: Ladbroke Grove. Map p 132.*

★★ Prince Charles Cinema

SOHO   One of London's best movie bargains, this independent theatre offers sing-along sessions of classic musicals, cult hits, mainstream classics, and first-run foreign flicks. *7 Leicester Place.* ☎ *020/7494-3654. www.princecharlescinema.com. Tickets £2.50–£6.50. Tube: Leicester Sq. Map p 132.*

Theatre

★★★ **The Old Vic** SOUTHBANK Except for a few wartime interruptions, this venerable theatre has been in continuous operation since 1818. The repertory troupe at "the actors" theatre has been a who's who of thespians over the years, including Sir Laurence Olivier, Dame Maggie Smith, and current artistic director Kevin Spacey. *The Cut.* ☎ *0844/871-7628. www.oldvic theatre.com. Tickets £10–£52.50. Tube: Waterloo. Map p 132.*

★★ **Open Air Theatre** MARYLEBONE The setting is idyllic, and the seating and acoustics are excellent at this Regent's Park venue. Presentations are mainly of Shakespeare's plays, usually in period costume. The season runs from June to mid-September. *Inner Circle, Regent's Park.* ☎ *0844/826-4242. www. openairtheatre.org. Tickets £14–£46. Tube: Baker St. Map p 132.*

★★ **Royal Court Theatre** CHELSEA This leader in provocative, cutting-edge theatre is home to the English Stage Company, which was formed to promote serious drama. *Sloane Sq.* ☎ *020/7565-5000. www.royal courttheatre.com. Tickets £10–£28. Tube: Sloane Sq. Map p 132.*

★★★ **Royal National Theatre** SOUTH BANK Home to one of the world's greatest stage companies, the Royal National presents the finest in world theatre, from classic drama to award-winning new plays, comedies, and musicals. *South Bank.* ☎ *020/7452-3000. www. nationaltheatre.org.uk. Tickets £10–£40. Tube: Waterloo or Charing Cross. Map p 132.*

★★★ **Shakespeare's Globe Theatre** SOUTH BANK This outdoor theatre is a replica of the Elizabethan original. You can choose to sit either on wooden benches (you can rent a cushion) or stand in front of the stage as a "groundling," just as theatre-goers did in the Bard's day. *21 New Globe Walk, Bankside.* ☎ *020/7902-1400. www.shakespeares-globe.org. Tickets £5 groundlings, £12–£34.50 gallery seats. Tube: London Bridge. Map p 132.*

Buying Theatre Tickets

You can buy advance tickets for most of London's entertainment venues through the theatres' websites or through **Ticketmaster** (www.ticketmaster.co.uk). Expect to pay a booking fee as high as £3.50 per ticket. Some concierges can set aside theatre tickets for hotel guests, so ask when booking your room.

For same-day, half-price tickets, your best bet is the **tkts booth** (www.tkts.co.uk) on the south side of Leicester Square, which opens at 10am (11am on Sun). Two boards list the day's available West End shows. The blockbusters will probably be difficult to obtain, but decent seats at all the longer-running productions should be available. Many theatres sell their own half-price standby tickets at the box office about an hour before curtain time.

Last Minute (www.lastminute.com) has plenty of good deals on theatre-dinner packages, but read the fine print carefully—some may have restrictions and booking fees that add up to more than £10.

West End Theatres

Adelphi Theatre, 409 Strand.
☎ 0844/412-4651

Aldwych Theatre, 49 Aldwych.
☎ 0870/400-0805

Apollo Theatre, 39 Shaftesbury Ave. ☎ 0870/890-1101

The Arts Theatre, 6–7 Great Newport St. ☎ 0870/060-1742

Cambridge Theatre, Earlham St.
☎ 0844/412-4652

Criterion Theatre, Piccadilly Circus. ☎ 0844/847-1778

Dominion Theatre, 268–269 Tottenham Court Rd.
☎ 0844/847-1775

Donmar Warehouse, 41 Earlham St. ☎ 0844/871-7624

Drury Lane Theatre Royal, Drury Lane. ☎ 0870/890-6002

Duchess Theatre, Catherine St.
☎ 0844/579-1973

Duke of York's Theatre, 104 St. Martin's Lane. ☎ 0870/060-6623

Fortune Theatre, Russell St.
☎ 0870/060-6626

Garrick Theatre, 2 Charing Cross Rd. ☎ 0870/890-1104

Gielgud Theatre, Shaftesbury Ave. ☎ 0844/482-5130

Harold Pinter Theatre, Panton St., ☎ 0870 060 6622

Her Majesty's Theatre, Haymarket. ☎ 0844/412-2707

London Palladium Theatre, 8 Argyll St. ☎ 0844/412-4655

Lyceum Theatre, 21 Wellington St. ☎ 0870/243-9000

Lyric Theatre, Shaftesbury Ave.
☎ 0844/412-4661

New London Theatre, Parker St.
☎ 0844/412-4654

Noël Coward Theatre (prev. Albery), 85 St. Martin's Lane.
☎ 0870/950-0920

Novello Theatre (prev. Strand), Aldwych. ☎ 0870/950-0935

Palace Theatre, 109–113 Shaftesbury Ave. ☎ 0870/890-0142

Phoenix Theatre, 110 Charing Cross. ☎ 0870/060-6629

Piccadilly Theatre, Denman St.
☎ 0844/412-6666

Playhouse Theatre, Northumberland Ave. ☎ 0870/060-6631

Prince Edward Theatre, 28 Old Compton St. ☎ 0844/482-5151

Prince of Wales Theatre, Coventry St. ☎ 0870/850-0393

Queen's Theatre, Shaftesbury Ave. (at Cambridge Circus).
☎ 0870/950-0930

St. Martin's Theatre, West St.
☎ 0844/499-1515

Savoy Theatre, Savoy Court, Strand. ☎ 0870/164-8787

Shaftesbury Theatre, 210 Shaftesbury Ave.
☎ 020/7379-5399

Trafalgar Studios (prev. Whitehall), 14 Whitehall.
☎ 0870/060-6632

Vaudeville Theatre, 404 Strand.
☎ 0870/890-1101

Wyndhams Theatre, Charing Cross Rd. ☎ 0844/482-5120 ●

Hotel Best Bets

The Thistle Piccadilly.

Best **Historic Hotel**
★★ Hazlitt's 1718, *6 Frith St., W1
(p 151)*

Best **Hotel for Victoriana**
★★ The Gore, *189 Queen's Gate,
SW7 (p 150)*

Best **Hotel for Clubbers**
★★ The Hoxton, *81 Gt. Eastern St.,
EC2 (p 151)*

Best **Luxury Hotel**
★★★ Claridge's, *Brook St., W1
(p 149)*

Most **Refined Atmosphere**
★★★ The Connaught, *Carlos Place,
W1 (p 149)*

Best **Hotel for Royal
Watching**
★★ The Rubens at the Palace, *39
Buckingham Palace Rd., SW1 (p 153)*

Best **Base for Museum-
Hopping**
★ The Gallery, *8–10 Queensberry
Place, SW7 (p 150)*

Previous page: Covent Garden Hotel.

Best **Views of the Thames**
★★ Park Plaza County Hall Hotel,
1 Addington St., SE1 (p 152)

Best **Chance to Get a Good
Package Deal**
★ The Rembrandt Hotel, *11
Thurloe Place, SW7 (p 152)*

Best **Placed for the Olympics**
★★ Town Hall, *8 Patriot Sq., E2
(p 154)*

Best **Hotel for Afternoon Tea**
★★ The Goring, *Beeston Place,
SW1 (p 150)*

Best **Value**
★ Mowbray Court Hotel, *28–32
Penywern Rd., SW5 (p 151)*

Best **Boutique Hotel**
★★★ Haymarket Hotel, *1 Suffolk
Place, SW1 (p 150)*

Best **Budget Choice**
★★★ Luna Simone Hotel, *47–49
Belgrave Rd., SW1 (p 151)*

Best **Family Hotel**
★ Lord Jim Hotel, *23–25 Penywern
St., SW5 (p 151)*

Most **Romantic Hotel**
★★★ San Domenico House, *29–31
Draycott Place, SW3 (p 153)*

Most **Quirky Decor**
★ Rough Luxe, *1 Birkenhead St.,
WC1 (p 153)*

Best **Bathrooms**
★★★ The Dorchester, *53 Park
Lane, W1 (p 149)*

Best **Business Hotel**
★ The Chamberlain Hotel, *130–135
Minories, EC3 (p 148)*

Best for **Theatre Buffs**
Thistle Piccadilly, *Coventry St., W1
(p 154)*

East End Hotels

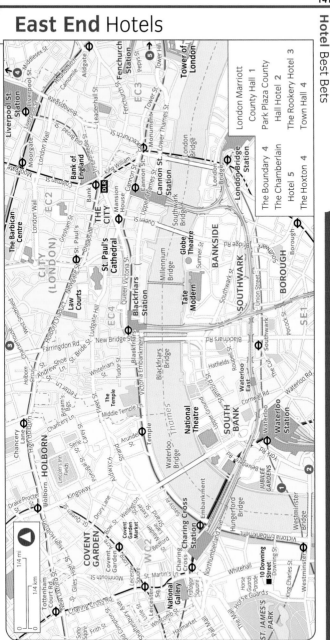

Hotel Best Bets

London Marriott
County Hall 1

Park Plaza County
Hall Hotel 2

The Rookery Hotel 3

Town Hall 4

The Boundary 4

The Chamberlain
Hotel 5

The Hoxton 4

Kensington Hotels

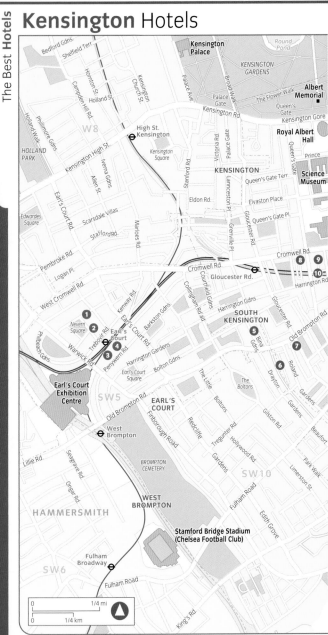

Kensington Palace

KENSINGTON GARDENS

Round Pond

The Flower Walk

Albert Memorial

Palace Gate

Queen's Gate

Kensington Rd.

Kensington Gore

High St. Kensington

Kensington Square

Royal Albert Hall

Prince

HOLLAND PARK

W8

Kensington High St.

KENSINGTON

Science Museum

Edwardes Square

Scarsdale Villas

Stafford Rd.

Eldon Rd.

Queen's Gate Terr.

Elvaston Place

Queen's Gate Pl.

Pembroke Rd.

Logan Pl.

Cromwell Rd.

Cromwell Rd.

Gloucester Rd.

8 **9**

10

Harrington Rd.

West Cromwell Rd.

1

Nevern Square

2

Earl's Court

4

3

Harrington Gdns.

SOUTH KENSINGTON

5

7

6

Earl's Court Exhibition Centre

SW5

EARL'S COURT

Bolton Gdns.

West Brompton

BROMPTON CEMETERY

WEST BROMPTON

SW10

HAMMERSMITH

Stamford Bridge Stadium (Chelsea Football Club)

Fulham Broadway

SW6

Fulham Road

King's Rd.

0   1/4 mi

0   1/4 km

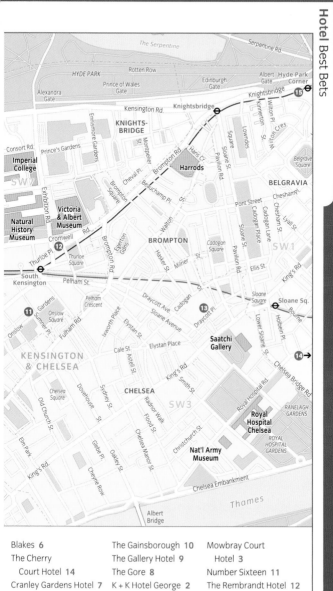

Blakes 6

The Cherry
Court Hotel 14

Cranley Gardens Hotel 7

The Cranley on
Bina Gardens Hotel 5

The Gainsborough 10

The Gallery Hotel 9

The Gore 8

K + K Hotel George 2

The Lanesborough 15

Lord Jim Hotel 4

Mowbray Court
Hotel 3

Number Sixteen 11

The Rembrandt Hotel 12

San Domenico House 13

Twenty Nevern Square 1

Notting Hill Hotels

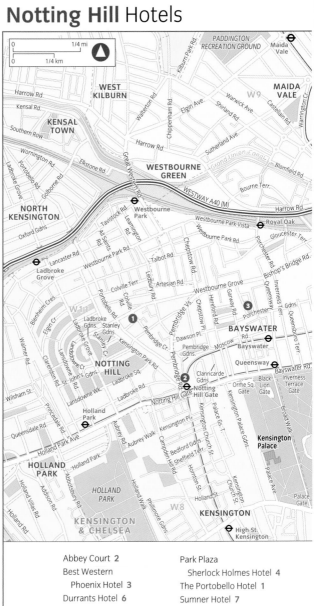

Abbey Court **2**
Best Western
  Phoenix Hotel **3**
Durrants Hotel **6**
The Goring **8**

Park Plaza
  Sherlock Holmes Hotel **4**
The Portobello Hotel **1**
Sumner Hotel **7**
Wigmore Court Hotel **5**

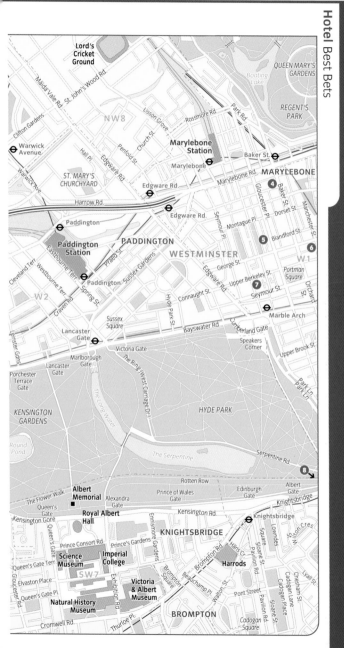

West End Hotels

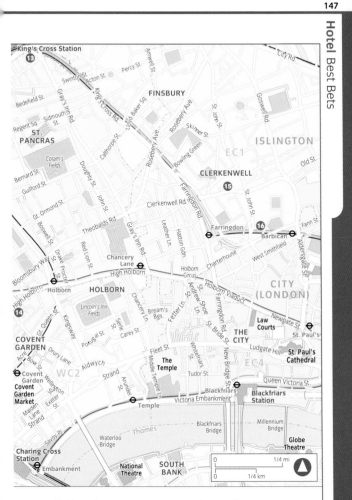

Claridge's **2**	Rough Luxe **13**
The Connaught **3**	The Royal Horseguards **6**
Covent Garden Hotel **9**	The Rubens at the Palace **5**
The Dorchester **1**	Sanderson London **11**
Fox & Anchor **16**	The Stafford London Kempinski **4**
Haymarket Hotel **7**	Thistle Piccadilly **8**
Hazlitt's 1718 **10**	Travelodge Covent Garden **14**
Luna Simone Hotel **5**	The Zetter **15**
Morgan Hotel **12**	

London Hotels A to Z

★ **kids Abbey Court** NOTTING HILL This four-floor Victorian town house has considerable charms, if you can get along without an elevator. *20 Pembridge Gardens, W4. ☎ 020/7221-7518. www.abbeycourt hotel.co.uk. 22 units. Doubles £135–£185. AE, DC, MC, V. Tube: Notting Hill Gate. Map p 144.*

★ **kids Best Western Phoenix Hotel** BAYSWATER You know what you're getting with Best Western—a good level of business comfort and decor. This one is a short walk from the transport links of Paddington and the green open spaces of Hyde Park. *1–8 Kensington Garden Sq., W2. ☎ 020/7229-2494. www.phoenixhotel.co.uk. 125 units. Doubles £132–£165. AE, DC, MC, V. Tube: Bayswater. Map p 144.*

★★ **Blakes** SOUTH KENSINGTON Still trendy after all these years, and still celebrated for its exotic and lavish decor. Alas, the prices do seem to get harder to swallow. *33 Roland Gardens, SW7. ☎ 020/7370-6701. www.blakes hotels.com. 47 units. Doubles £325–£375. AE, DC, MC, V. Tube: Gloucester Rd. Map p 142.*

The Pavilion Suite, Claridge's.

★★ **The Boundary** EAST END Terence Conran, always up with the latest trends, has joined the great London push eastward with the opening of this hotel in a converted East End warehouse. The decor is as sharp as you'd expect and there's a good roof terrace restaurant. *2–4 Boundary St., E2. ☎ 020/7729-1051. www.theboundary.co.uk. 17 units. Doubles £140–£280. AE, DC, MC, V. Tube: Shoreditch High St. Map p 141.*

★ **kids The Chamberlain Hotel** EAST END Business travelers enjoy the easy access to the City, and Tower of London lovers couldn't be happier with the location of this modern hotel in a converted Georgian building. *130–135 Minories, EC3. ☎ 020/7373-3232. www.fullers hotels.com. 64 units. Doubles £90–£145. AE, DC, MC, V. Tube: Tower Hill. Map p 141.*

★★ **kids The Cherry Court Hotel** PIMLICO They don't come much cheaper than this pleasant hotel, at least not with the same degree of cleanliness and comfort. *23 Hugh St., SW1. ☎ 020/7828-2840. www.cherrycourthotel.co.uk. 12 units. Doubles £60. Add 5% for*

The Connaught's Coburg Bar.

credit cards. AE, MC, V. Tube: Victoria. Map p 142.

★★★ kids Claridge's MAYFAIR
This redoubtable London institution, close to Bond Street's shopping, has been the final word in elegance for decades. Rooms are spacious and service is impeccable. *Brook St., W1.* 020/7629-8860. www.claridges. co.uk. 203 units. Doubles £374–£461. AE, DC, MC, V. Tube: Bond St. Map p 146.

★★★ The Connaught MAY-
FAIR With all the stately grandeur of an old-style gentlemen's club, The Connaught is as gloriously dignified as the neighborhood around it. A major refurbishment has added modern touches. Go for tea if you can't afford the steep rates. *Carlos Place, W1.* 020/7499-7070. www. the-connaught.co.uk. 123 units. Doubles £366–£450. AE, DC, MC, V. Tube: Bond St. Map p 146.

★★★ kids Covent Garden Hotel SOHO Big beds, relatively large rooms, and deft English decor make this popular hotel one of the best in Soho. The downside: The neighborhood gets as rowdy at night as it is touristy during the day. *10 Monmouth St., WC2.* 020/ 7806-1000. www.firmdale.com. 50

units. Doubles £250–£355. AE, DC, MC, V. Tube: Covent Garden. Map p 146.

★ kids Cranley Gardens Hotel
SOUTH KENSINGTON Good prices in a great neighborhood. The decor is a bit faux country-house, but it's a cheerful, pleasant family-owned hotel made up of four Victorian houses. *8 Cranley Gardens, SW7.* 020/7373-3232. www.cranley gardenshotel.com. 85 units. Doubles £105–£115. AE, MC, V. Tube: Gloucester Rd. Map p 142.

★★ kids The Cranley on Bina Gardens Hotel SOUTH KENSING-TON Very romantic (the classic decor is laid over gorgeous period details), this hotel boasts a rooftop terrace, high ceilings, and free Wi-Fi in every bedroom—all in a quiet but convenient location. *10–12 Bina Gardens, SW5.* 020/7373-0123. www. thecranley.com. 39 units. Doubles £135–£175. AE, MC, V. Tube: Gloucester Rd. Map p 142.

★★★ The Dorchester MAY-
FAIR This opulent gem welcomes kings and commoners with equal panache (so long as the commoners have the requisite amount of cash, of course). Elegant decor, first-rate amenities, and to-die-for bathrooms. *53 Park Lane, W1.* 020/7629-8888. www.thedorchester.com. 250 units. Doubles £255–£495. AE, DC, MC, V. Tube: Hyde Park Corner. Map p 146.

★★ kids Durrants Hotel
MARYLEBONE This clubby hotel offers good value and a great location close to Oxford Street's shopping and the Wallace Collection. *George St., W1.* 020/7935-8131. www.durrantshotel.co.uk. 92 units. Doubles £130–£216. AE, MC, V. Tube: Bond St. Map p 144.

Fox & Anchor CLERKENWELL
Above a traditional English pub—all etched glass and brass fittings—are

Elegant sitting room at the Covent Garden Hotel.

six cozy, classy rooms, with wooden floors, giant TVs, and free-standing beds. The pub kitchen serves up giant carnivorous breakfasts using fresh produce from the nearby meat market. *115 Charterhouse St., EC1.* ☎ *020/7550-1000. www.foxandanchor.com. 6 units. Doubles £112–£280 w/breakfast. AE, DC, MC, V. Tube: Barbican. Map p 146.*

★ **kids** **The Gainsborough** SOUTH KENSINGTON A stone's throw from the Natural History Museum (p 44), this hotel offers well-appointed rooms at a decent price. *7–11 Queensberry Place, SW7.* ☎ *020/7838-1700. www.hotelgainsborough.co.uk. 49 units. Doubles £135–£159 w/breakfast. AE, DC, MC, V. Tube: S. Kensington. Map p 142.*

★ **kids** **The Gallery Hotel** SOUTH KENSINGTON This Victorian hotel's pluses include small, comfortable rooms with attractive marble bathrooms, and great breakfasts. *8–10 Queensberry Place, SW7.* ☎ *020/7970-1805. www.eeh.co.uk/hotel_gallery. 37 units. Doubles £101–£123 w/breakfast. AE, DC, MC, V. Tube: S. Kensington. Map p 142.*

★★ **kids** **The Gore** SOUTH KENSINGTON Every room inside this gorgeous re-creation of an early Victorian hotel is individually decorated with fine antiques. *189 Queen's Gate, SW7.* ☎ *020/7584-6601. www.gorehotel.co.uk. 50 units. Doubles £186–£498. AE, DC, MC, V. Tube: Gloucester Rd. Map p 142.*

★★ **kids** **The Goring** PIMLICO Although it is near Victoria Station, this hotel has the feel of a country house, with a big walled garden, charming public spaces, and excellent afternoon teas. *Beeston Place, SW1.* ☎ *020/7396-9000. www.goringhotel.co.uk. 71 units. Doubles £230–£649. AE, DC, MC, V. Tube: Victoria. Map p 144.*

★★★ **kids** **Haymarket Hotel** WEST END The Haymarket's location is perfect for West End fun, and the decor is worth dropping by to gawk at. It's not cheap, but neither is putting in a fabulous pool in central London. *1 Suffolk Place, SW1.* ☎ *020/7470-4000. www.firmdale.com. 50 units. Doubles £250–£350. AE, MC, V. Tube: Piccadilly Circus. Map p 146.*

★★ Hazlitt's 1718 SOHO
Favored by the literary set, the 18th-century-flavored Hazlitt's feels more like a boarding house than a hotel. There's no elevator. *6 Frith St., W1.* ☎ *020/7434-1771. www.hazlitts hotel.com. 23 units. Doubles £205–£330. AE, DC, MC, V. Tube: Tottenham Court Rd. Map p 146.*

★★ The Hoxton SHOREDITCH
Right at the heart of the Hoxton/Shoreditch nightlife scene, this does a roaring trade with clubbers who don't want to (or can't) drag themselves home at the end of the evening. The rooms are simple, clean, and cheap, and it has a fun vibe. *81 Great Eastern St., London EC2.* ☎ *020/7550-1000. www.hoxton hotels.com. 205 units. Doubles £49–£199 w/breakfast. AE, DC, MC, V. Tube: Old St. Map p 141.*

★★ kids K + K Hotel George
KENSINGTON   Part of a popular European chain, this is a good bet for elegance and convenience at an affordable rate (depending on the season). Enjoy the garden when weather permits. *1–15 Templeton Place, SW5.* ☎ *020/7598-8700. www.kkhotels.com. 154 units. Doubles £148–£175. AE, DC, MC, V. Tube: Earl's Court. Map p 142.*

★★★ kids The Lanesborough
KNIGHTSBRIDGE   Housed in a former hospital building, this grand Regency-style hotel features state-of-the-art amenities—and your very own butler. *Hyde Park Corner, SW1.* ☎ *020/7259-5599. www. lanesborough.com. 95 units. Doubles £395–£455. AE, DC, MC, V. Tube: Hyde Park Corner. Map p 142.*

★ kids London Marriott County Hall SOUTH BANK   You can't beat the views of Big Ben and Parliament from this chain's rooms, though the prices are steep. *County Hall, SE1.* ☎ *020/7928-5200. www. marriotthotels.com. 186 units. Doubles £225–£305. AE, DC, MC, V. Tube: Waterloo. Map p 141.*

★ kids Lord Jim Hotel EARL'S COURT   Known for its attractive package deals, this budget hotel offers plainly but pleasantly decorated rooms; families will fit easily inside the bigger ones. *23–25 Penywern Rd., SW5.* ☎ *020/7370-6071. www.thelordsgroup.co.uk. 50 units. Doubles £100–£109 w/breakfast. AE, DC, MC, V. Tube: Earl's Court. Map p 142.*

★★★ kids Luna Simone Hotel
VICTORIA   Amid the great swamp of cheap accommodation surrounding Victoria Station, the Luna Simone stands head and shoulders above its rivals. The rooms are bijou but everything within is neat and tidy and the staff are supremely friendly. *47–49 Belgrave Rd., SW1.* ☎ *020/7834-5897. www.luna simonehotel.com. 36 units. Doubles £95–£120 w/breakfast. AE, DC, MC, V. Tube: Victoria. Map p 146.*

★ kids Morgan Hotel BLOOMSBURY   The family-run Morgan features well-kept Georgian-style rooms. It's an old favorite of Anglophiles who can't get enough of the nearby British Museum (p 26). *24 Bloomsbury St., WC1.* ☎ *020/7636-3735. www.morganhotel.co.uk. 21 units. Doubles £125 w/breakfast. MC, V. Tube: Tottenham Court Rd. Map p 146.*

★ kids Mowbray Court Hotel
EARL'S COURT   This spotless budget hotel, run by a friendly Irish family, features basic rooms, some without private bathrooms. *28–32 Penywern Rd., SW5.* ☎ *020/7370-2316. www.mowbraycourthotel. co.uk. 90 units. Doubles £76–£86 w/ breakfast. AE, DC, MC, V. Tube: Earl's Court. Map p 142.*

★ **kids** **Number Sixteen** SOUTH KENSINGTON   This modernized Victorian town-house hotel is popular with Americans, quiet, and in a fun neighborhood. *16 Sumner Place, SW7.* ☎ *020/7589-5232. www. numbersixteenhotel.co.uk. 42 units. Doubles £230–£320. AE, DC, MC, V. Tube: S. Kensington. Map p 142.*

★★ **kids** **Park Plaza County Hall Hotel** WATERLOO   The cheap alternative to the Marriott if you want to stay in the superbly well-located County Hall building on the south bank of the Thames. The rooms are a good size and there are plenty of amenities. *1 Addington St., SE1.* ☎ *020/7034-4820. www.park plazacountyhall.com. 398 units. Doubles £154–£195. AE, DC, MC, V. Tube: Baker St. Map p 141.*

★ **kids** **Park Plaza Sherlock Holmes Hotel** MARYLEBONE   This modern boutique hotel is on Baker Street near the (imaginary) home of the fictional sleuth, but it's hardly Sherlockian in decor. It's a short walk to Regent's Park and Oxford Street. *108 Baker St., W1.* ☎ *020/7486-6161. www.parkplaza sherlockholmes.com. 119 units.*

Doubles £129–£164. AE, DC, MC, V. Tube: Baker St. Map p 144.

★★★ **The Portobello Hotel** NOTTING HILL   Sumptuously decorated guest rooms are the hallmark of this trendy hotel—a hit with the music and modeling set—located near Portobello Road. *22 Stanley Gardens, W1.* ☎ *020/7727-2777. www.portobello-hotel.co.uk. 24 units. Doubles £195–£245 w/break-fast. AE, DC, MC, V. Tube: Notting Hill Gate. Map p 144.*

★ **kids** **The Rembrandt Hotel** SOUTH KENSINGTON   This solid tourist hotel across from the V&A (p 30) is popular with groups because of its package deals and many rooms. *11 Thurloe Place, SW7.* ☎ *020/7589-8100. www.sarova. com/rembrandt. 195 units. Doubles £149–£219 w/breakfast. AE, DC, MC, V. Tube: S. Kensington. Map p 142.*

★★ **The Rookery Hotel** EAST END   A sure-footed evocation of a bygone era, The Rookery is set on the edge of the City; each room is individually decorated with rare antiques. *Peter's Lane, Cowcross St., EC1.* ☎ *020/7336-0931. www. rookeryhotel.com. 33 units. Doubles*

The Silk Room at The Goring.

The Thistle Piccadilly.

£135–£165. AE, DC, MC, V. Tube: Farringdon. Map p 141.

★ **Rough Luxe** BLOOMSBURY Behind the traditional Georgian town house facade is something much more kooky. As the name suggests, the hotel's look is a mixture of the rough (bare brick, distressed walls) and the luxurious (modern art and antiques). The result is a cross between a guesthouse and an art gallery. *1 Birkenhead St., WC1.* ☎ *020/7837-5338. 9 units. Doubles £155–£210 w/breakfast. AE, MC, V. Tube: King's Cross. Map p 146.*

★★ kids **The Royal Horse-guards** WESTMINSTER Right at the heart of royal London, this may be the best-located hotel in town. It's less stuffy than you might think—rooms are modern and rather snazzy-looking—but it still makes for a quintessential English experience. *2 Whitehall Court, SW1.* ☎ *0871/376-9033. www. guoman.com/theroyalhorseguards. 281 units. Doubles £198–£300. AE, DC, MC, V. Tube: Embankment. Map p 146.*

★★ kids **The Rubens at the Palace** VICTORIA Traditional English hospitality combined with the latest in creature comforts, just across the road from the Royal Mews. The Royal Rooms have the most atmosphere. *39 Buckingham Palace Rd., SW1.* ☎ *020/7834-6600, 877/955-1515 in the U.S. www. rubenshotel.com. 161 units. Doubles £149–£199. AE, DC, MC, V. Tube: Victoria. Map p 146.*

★★ **Sanderson London** WEST END If glam is your thing, this is the hotel for you. Inside it's all polished steel, lip-shaped sofas, and Philippe Starck furniture. It has a bit of a party vibe, but the rooms are large, quiet, and luxurious, and there are plenty of opportunities to relax at the spa or Japanese roof garden. *50 Berners St., W1.* ☎ *020/7300-1400. www.sanderson london.com. 150 units. Doubles £225–£405 w/breakfast. AE, DC, MC, V. Tube: Goodge St. Map p 146.*

★★★ **San Domenico House** CHELSEA An exquisite hotel delivering divine Italian luxury at its most romantic and English-accented. *29–31 Draycott Place, SW3.* ☎ *020/ 7581-5757. www.sandomenico house.com. 16 units. Doubles £235– £255. AE, DC, MC, V. Tube: Sloane Sq. Map p 142.*

★★ kids **The Stafford London Kempinski** MAYFAIR This gorgeous 18th-century hotel, set in a grand old neighborhood, combines English country style with modern amenities. *St. James's Place,*

The Best Hotels

SW1. ☎ 020/7493-0111. www.the staffordhotel.co.uk. 81 units. Doubles £212–£432. AE, DC, MC, V. Tube: Green Park. Map p 146.

★★ **Sumner Hotel** MARBLE ARCH One of London's best small, reasonably priced hotels, the Sumner is well-loved by clued-in visitors. *54 Upper Berkeley St., W1. ☎ 020/7723-2244. www.thesumner.com. 20 units. Doubles £158–£215 w/ breakfast. AE, DC, MC, V. Tube: S. Kensington. Map p 144.*

kids Thistle Piccadilly PICCADILLY There's no better location for those who want to hit the theatres, clubs, and restaurants of the West End. Check the website for packages and promotions. *Coventry St., W1. ☎ 0871/376-9031. www.thistle.com. 92 units. Doubles £119–£251 w/breakfast. AE, DC, MC, V. Tube: Piccadilly. Map p 146.*

★★ **Town Hall** BETHNAL GREEN The opening of this design-tastic place in the former Bethnal Green Town Hall has further confirmed the East End's status as London's most up-and-coming area. It's as swanky and cool (and expensive) as anything in central London, with a spa, a pool, and one of the hottest restaurants around, Viajante. *8 Patriot Sq., E2. ☎ 020/7871-0460. www.townhallhotel.com. 98 units. Doubles £174–£201. AE, DC, MC, V. Tube: Bethnal Green. Map p 141.*

kids Travelodge Covent Garden COVENT GARDEN It's in a dreadful building, but the rooms are clean and serviceable, and the

neighborhood rocks. And what you'll save on lodging you can spend at the theatres and cafes on Drury Lane. *10 Drury Lane, WC2. ☎ 020/7208-9988. www.travelodge.co.uk. 163 units. Doubles £65–£105. AE, MC, V. Tube: Covent Garden. Map p 146.*

★★ **Twenty Nevern Square** EARL'S COURT Elegant European–Asian decor, a full range of amenities, and a garden make this one of the more sumptuous B&Bs in London. *20 Nevern Sq., SW5. ☎ 020/7565-9555. www.twentynevernsquare.co.uk. 20 units. Doubles £79–£195 w/breakfast. AE, DC, MC, V. Tube: Earl's Court. Map p 142.*

kids Wigmore Court Hotel MARYLEBONE Clean, friendly, and well-located, the Wigmore Court is a favorite of the budget-conscious and is well-suited to family groups. *23 Gloucester Place, W1. ☎ 020/7935-0928. www.wigmore-hotel.co.uk. 16 units. Doubles £75–£120 w/breakfast. MC, V. Tube: Marble Arch. Map p 144.*

★★★ **The Zetter** CLERKENWELL A great addition to the City's accommodation options, this is artsy and funky—places around here are usually businessy and dull. The rooms in the five-story converted Victorian warehouse are a little small but tastefully done. Those at the top have panoramic views of the skyline. *St. John's Sq., 86–88 Clerkenwell Rd., EC1. ☎ 020/7324-4444. www.thezetter.com. 59 units. Doubles £153–£360. AE, DC, MC, V. Tube: Farringdon. Map p 146.* ●

The
Savvy Traveler

Before You Go

Government Tourist Offices (Visit Britain)

In the U.S.: Visit Britain, 551 Fifth Ave., 7th Floor, New York, NY 10176 (☎ **800/462-2748**). **In Canada:** Visit Britain, 5915 Airport Rd., Suite 120, Mississauga, Ontario L4V 1T1 (☎ **905/405-1840**). **In Ireland:** Visit Britain, 18–19 College Green, Dublin 2 (☎ **01/670-8000**). **In Australia:** Visit Britain, Level 16, Gateway, 1 Macquarie Place, Sydney, NSW 2000 (☎ **029/377-4400**). **In New Zealand:** Visit Britain, Fay Rich White Building, 151 Queen St., Auckland 1 (☎ **09/303-1446**). The best place for information, regardless of your home country, is on the Web at **www.visitbritain.com** or **www.visitlondon.com**. You can download PDF brochures and maps, or have them mailed to a U.K. or U.S. address, or ask any question about the city by filling out the online contact form at **www.visitlondon.com/contact-us**.

The Best Time to Go

Although prices are highest in spring and summer, the weather is best then (though you should be prepared for showers at any time). Sunny and warm August is a sensible time to visit because many Londoners go on vacation and London's notorious traffic lightens up (slightly). The only problem is all those extra tourists. Fares are cheapest between November and March, Christmas and New Year excepted. The city's museum and theatre scenes are still in full swing in winter, but the city can get dark and chilly and bleak. September and early October can be gray and rainy, too, but most gardens are still in bloom.

Previous page: Big Ben.

Festivals & Special Events

JANUARY. The **New Year's Day Parade** (☎ 020/8566-8586; www.londonparade.co.uk) sees an estimated 10,000 performers march, dance, and play their way through London's streets, from Parliament Square to Green Park, to celebrate the start of the year with what may seem to many inappropriate enthusiasm (particularly if they're still recovering from the night before).

FEBRUARY. **Chinese New Year** is celebrated in Soho's Chinatown with the requisite dancing lions and red confetti. The **Great Spitalfields Pancake Race** (www.alternativearts.co.uk/events) on Shrove Tuesday (called Pancake Day in the U.K.) is a bizarre old tradition that combines tossed pancakes and teams of runners.

MARCH. One of the month's best-loved events is the **Oxford & Cambridge Boat Race** from Putney Bridge to Mortlake (**www.theboatrace.org**). There are a number of good pubs and vantage points along the 4-mile route, but Hammersmith and Putney bridges are the best places to watch. March also sees London's large Irish community celebrate **St. Patrick's Day** with floats, musicians, plenty of Guinness, and a non-stop party from Hyde Park to Trafalgar Square (www.london.gov.uk/stpatricksday).

APRIL. Tens of thousands of people run the **London Marathon** (www.virginlondonmarathon.com) every year. The 26-mile course runs from Greenwich Park to St. James's Park. The best views are from Victoria Embankment.

MAY. A difficult ticket to get hold of, the **Chelsea Flower Show**

(☎ 0844/338-7506; +44 121 767-4063 from outside the U.K.; www.rhs.org.uk) is a wonderful spectacle, packed with creative garden displays.

JUNE. The **Royal Academy Summer Exhibition** (www.royalacademy.org.uk), the world's largest public art display, showcases the works of artists of every genre and caliber. **The Queen's Official Birthday** (Elizabeth II was actually born in April) is honored with a carriage ride, a gun salute, and **Trooping the Colour** at Horse Guards Parade. On **London Open Weekend** (www.opensquares.org), a number of gardens usually available only to private keyholders are opened to an envious public. **Royal Ascot** (www.ascot.co.uk) is the big social horse event of the year, a time when the upper classes dust off their chapeaus and take part in the old tradition of betting on horses while dressed to the nines. The **Lawn Tennis Championships at Wimbledon** (☎ 020/8971-2473/8944-1066; www.wimbledon.com) need no introduction, but you will require a very-hard-to-get ticket (see "Spectator Sports," later in this chapter).

JULY. **The Proms** (☎ 020/7589-8212; www.bbc.co.uk/proms), formally known as the BBC Sir Henry Wood Promenade Concerts, held in and outside the Royal Albert Hall, are the annual joy of London's classical music lovers. The season runs from mid-July to mid-September. There are now **Pride Parades** held across the country, but the capital's version, held on the first Sunday in July, is still the biggest event in the gay party calendar. The flamboyant procession heads from Baker Street to Trafalgar Square (www.pridelondon.org).

AUGUST. The **Notting Hill Carnival** (www.thenottinghillcarnival.com), the largest street festival in Europe,

is held in and around Portobello Road. Expect crowds, beer, and spicy Caribbean cuisine.

SEPTEMBER. During the 2-day **Open House** (www.londonopenhouse.org), hundreds of usually inaccessible architectural gems are opened to the public.

OCTOBER. At the 125-year-old **Pearly Kings & Queens Harvest Festival** (☎ 020/7766-1100; www.pearlysociety.co.uk), the descendants of London's cockney costermongers (market traders) dress in costumes covered with pearly buttons and gather at a church service at St. Martin-in-the-Fields for charity—and to show off their button-sewing prowess. Floats and carriages make their way from Mansion House to the Royal Courts of Justice and back again during **The Lord Mayor's Show** (www.lordmayorsshow.org).

NOVEMBER. **Guy Fawkes Night** commemorates the thwarted destruction of Parliament with bonfires and fireworks all over London. Book a couple of spins on the London Eye (p 11, ⑥) after dark so you can see London's sky lit up from near and far.

DECEMBER. For the horse-mad, there is no better fun than the **International Show-jumping Championships** (☎ 020/7370-8202; www.olympiashowjumping.com) in Kensington. Thousands of Londoners see in the **New Year** by finding vantage points for the spectacular fireworks display that takes place on and around the London Eye as Big Ben's bongs sound.

The Weather

London's notorious (man-made) pea-soup fogs have long been eradicated, but a tendency toward showers and gray skies is ever-present—particularly November through March, when the sun shows its face only briefly. The weather can be

LONDON'S AVERAGE TEMPERATURE & RAINFALL

	JAN	FEB	MAR	APR	MAY	JUNE
Daily Temp. (°F)	43	44	50	55	63	68
Daily Temp. (°C)	6	7	10	13	17	20
Avg. Rainfall (in/mm)	3/54	1.5/40	1.5/37	1.5/37	1.8/46	1.8/45

	JULY	AUG	SEPT	OCT	NOV	DEC
Daily Temp. (°F)	72	70	66	57	50	44
Daily Temp. (°C)	22	21	19	14	10	7
Avg. Rainfall (in/mm)	2.2/59	2.3/59	1.9/49	2.2/57	2.5/64	1.9/48

fickle, and experiencing all four seasons in the span of a single day is common in all seasons except winter. The general climate is relatively mild, never going much above 75°F (24°C) or below 40°F (4°C). There are no great extremes, except for a few unpleasant dog days in summer (when a temperature of 80°F/27°C is considered a heat wave) and a snowfall or two during the short, dark days of a bleak midwinter.

For the local London forecast go to **uk.weather.com** for up-to-date weather information.

Useful Websites

- **www.londontown.com**: Offers specials on hotels, sells theatre tickets, and has lots of useful information.
- **www.royal.gov.uk**: If you're a royal watcher, or are just looking for information, trivia, or anything else about the British royal family, direct your browser to this site.
- **www.tfl.gov.uk**: London Transport's website is the source of information on London's public transportation system, including the Tube, buses, and ferries.
- **www.thisislondon.co.uk**: The *London Evening Standard*'s website is a good source of current entertainment and restaurant information.

- **www.timeout.com**: The weekly magazine has cultural event listings, as well as information on entertainment, restaurants, and nightlife.
- **www.visitbritain.com**: Great Britain's official tourist website features lots of useful information and trip-planning advice.
- **www.visitlondon.com**: London's official website features loads of information and lets you book hotels, buy discount passes, and more.

Cellphones

If you have a GSM phone, you can make and receive calls in London, though you will accrue whopping roaming charges.

International visitors can buy a pay-as-you-go cellphone (or, if you have an unlocked GSM phone, a SIM-only tariff) at any phone store in London. This gives you a local number and minutes that can be topped up with phone cards that can be purchased at newsagents. O2 and Vodafone are the best service networks.

Your hotel may be able to rent you a cellphone while in London, though it won't be cheap; inquire before you arrive. North Americans can rent one before leaving home from **InTouch USA** (☎ **800/872-7626;** www.intouchglobal.com).

Car Rentals

In a word—don't. Driving in London is a royal pain and I strongly recommend against it. You're far better off sticking to public transportation when you take into account the congestion fee (a charge of £10 for entering a large area of the city from 7am–6:30pm), the dreadful traffic, the dearth of street parking, and the astronomically high price of petrol. If you still want to rent a vehicle, all major car-rental companies operate in the U.K., and cars can be picked up at any of the major airports.

Getting **There**

By Plane

Air Canada, American, British Airways, Continental, Delta, Northwest, United, and Virgin Atlantic Airways offer nonstop service from various locations in the U.S. and Canada to London's major airports. Qantas offers a daily service to London from Sydney and Melbourne.

London is served by five airports. **London Heathrow Airport** (☎ 0844/335-1801; www.heathrow airport.com), located 15 miles west of London, is the largest. The fastest way into town is the **Heathrow Express** (☎ 0845/600-1515; www. heathrowexpress.com) train to Paddington Station (15 min.; £18). You can also take a cheaper ride on the Tube's Piccadilly Line into Central London (40 min.; £5). Black cabs cost roughly £50–£60 to the center of the city.

The city's second airport, **Gatwick Airport** (☎ 0844/335-1802; +44 208/528-2900 outside the U.K.; www.gatwickairport.com) is 25 miles south of London. The fastest (and best) way to get to the city is via the **Gatwick Express** (☎ 0845/ 850-1530; www.gatwickexpress. com) trains to Victoria Station (30 min.; £17.90). A taxi ride into London usually takes an hour, and can cost more than £125.

Stansted (☎ 0870/000-0303) and **Luton** (☎ 0158/240-5100) airports handle mostly short-hop flights on bargain airlines (usually easyJet and Ryanair) from European and U.K. destinations. Both are more than 50 miles from London. To get from Stansted to the city, take a **Stansted Express** (☎ 0845/850-0150;** www.stanstedexpress.com) train to Liverpool Street Station (45 min.; £20). From Luton, take **Greenline bus no. 757** (☎ 0870/608-2608;** www.greenline.co.uk) to Victoria Station (1 hr. 39 min.; £15).

The fifth and final airport, **London City** (☎ 020/7646-0088; www.londoncityairport.com) is by far the smallest and the only one actually in Greater London. It services mainly business travelers. **DLR** trains run every 10 minutes to Bank Tube Station (23 min.; £5). A taxi to the center of town should cost around £20.

By Train

The **Eurostar** provides direct train services between Paris (2¼ hr.) or Brussels (2 hr.) and London's St. Pancras Station in King's Cross. In London, make reservations for Eurostar at ☎ 0843/218-6186. (Outside the U.K., call +44 123/361-7575.) You can make advance train reservations from any country at **www. eurostar.com**. King's Cross/St. Pancras has six Tube line connections (Piccadilly, Circle, Hammersmith & City, Metropolitan, Northern, and Victoria), as well as overland trains connecting to the north and Scotland. Buses and taxis are readily available just outside the station.

National Rail (☎ 08457/48-4950; www.nationalrail.co.uk) trains connect just about every major city in the U.K. to one of London's major train stations (Charing Cross, Liverpool, Paddington, Victoria, King's Cross, Waterloo, and Euston). All major train stations in Central London have Tube stations and offer easy access to buses and taxis.

By Bus

Bus connections to Britain from the Continent, using the Channel Tunnel (Chunnel) or ferry services, are generally not very comfortable and take as long as 8 hours, but you can get a round-trip to Paris for as little as £38. Do check ahead to make sure your bus has a bathroom onboard; some do not. **National Express** (☎ 0871/781-8178; www.national express.com) long-haul buses traveling within the U.K. and to the Continent generally use centrally located Victoria Coach Station as their terminus. The bus station is on the corner of Buckingham Palace Road and Elizabeth Street, a few minutes' walk from the main Victoria Station, serviced by Sputhern, Southeastern, Gatwick Express, and London Underground trains, and a stop on the Underground's District and Circle lines. Victoria Station has a taxi stand and is the terminus for many local city buses.

Getting **Around**

Discount Travel Passes

Explaining the prices and passes for London's public transport is a Byzantine exercise worthy of a *Monty Python* skit. Sorting through the various prices for 1-day and 7-day passes, the rules for different ages of children, prices with and without museum discount passes, peak and off-peak travel time, and the different costs of tickets among the outer travel zones in London is exceedingly complicated. Worse, the system is always trying new "improvements" in the vain hope of softening the blow of the basic £4 one-way Tube ticket in Zones 1 and 2, even while plotting the latest fare increase. If you want the very latest prices, and the possibility of grasping the latest twist in pricing and discounted travel, settle in for a long read at the **Transport for London** website at **www.tfl.gov.uk**. You can also pick up the booklet given away at all Tube stations that attempts to explain it all.

One way to cut through all the variables is the efficient and penny-wise **Oyster Card,** a prepaid, reusable smartcard that deducts the cost of a trip each time you touch your card to the yellow card reader found on all public transportation (including the Docklands Light Railway and National Rail). You pay a one-time, refundable charge of £5 for the plastic card, but you'll save that on your first few trips with the Oyster Card's discounted fares (£1.90 for a one-way, off-peak Tube trip in Zones 1 and 2, rising to £2.70 for Zones 1 to 6). They can be purchased at any Tube station or online. It is not necessary to register the card. To retrieve the £5 card cost plus any money left on it, simply present it at any Tube station and they will refund your money on the spot.

Another nice feature is that the Oyster Card tops out each day at a certain price: The cap on Oyster Card charges per day on buses is

£4; on off-peak tube trips in zones 1 and 2 it's £6.60 (during peak times it's £8). For more information, check out **https://oyster.tfl.gov.uk/oyster/entry.do**.

London Transport's **Travelcards** offer unlimited use of buses, Underground, and Overground rail services in Greater London. A **1-day off-peak Travelcard** for Zones 1 and 2 costs £6.60 for adults, £3 for children aged 5–15 (for Zones 1 to 6 £8 and £3 respectively), which means you save £1.30 on one round-trip on the Tube in Zones 1 and 2. A **7-day Travelcard** for Zones 1 and 2 costs £27.60 adults, £13.80 children aged 5–15.

Up to four children aged 16 and under, accompanied by a ticket-holding adult, may travel free. Children aged 14–16 need a photo ID card, which can be purchased at a Tube station or online at either **www.tfl.gov.uk** or **www.london travelpass.com**.

You can buy Travelcards and Oyster Cards at machines (using cash or credit cards) in Underground stations. Surf the very comprehensive London Transport website at **www.tfl.gov.uk** for more information on discount options.

By Underground (Tube)

The world's first underground train (known today as the Underground or **the Tube**) was born in London in 1863. Stifling, overpopulated cars, sudden mysterious stops, and arbitrary line closures make the Tube the sacred monster of London's commuters. Love it or loathe it, it's the lifeblood of the city, and its 11 lines (plus the Docklands Light Railway to Greenwich and the London overground network covering much of eastern and southern suburbia) are usually the quickest way to get around the city.

All Tube stations are clearly marked with a red circle and blue crossbar. Routes are color-coded. The Tube runs daily, except Christmas, from 5:30am to 12:30am (until 11:30pm Sun), after which you must take a night bus or taxi. Fares start at £4 for a single journey without an Oyster card within Zones 1 and 2 (the ones most frequented by tourists). Buy your ticket, Oyster, or Travelcard from a machine inside the Tube station (most take credit cards) or from a clerk at a ticket window. Insert your ticket it into the turnstile, and then retrieve it and hold onto it—it must be reinserted into the turnstile or presented to a clerk when you exit the station at your destination or you'll pay a fine of £20; repeat offenders can get hit with as much as a £1,000 fine. Oyster card users should always touch their card as you leave the station (even if there is no gate) or the maximum charge will be applied.

Study a Tube map (available at most major Tube stations) or consult the indispensable *London A to Z* street atlas (pick it up at any London bookstore or newsstand) to find the stop nearest your destination. Note that you may have to switch lines in order to get from one destination to another. You can also download Tube maps and apps onto most smartphones. For more information on the Tube, check out **www.tfl.gov.uk**.

By Bus

The city's bus system has many advantages over the Tube: With the bus lanes and the (slight) reduction in traffic from the city's congestion charge, above-ground travel is almost as efficient as the Underground. It also costs about half as much as the Tube for adults—particularly as it's a flat fare right across town—and is completely free for children under 16 (provided they have the appropriate photocard), offering the potential for big savings

The Savvy Traveler

for large family groups. And, it has to be said, you get far better views of the city from buses than from Tubes. The city's red double-decker buses are a tourist attraction in their own right. Route maps are available at major Tube stations (Euston, Victoria, and Piccadilly Circus, to name a few) or online at **www.tfl.gov.uk**. You can also call a 24-hour hotline (☎ **0843/7222-1234**) for schedule and fare information.

Fares are a flat rate £2.20 for adults per journey, regardless of its length. Oyster Cards and Travelcards are valid on buses. A single bus fare using the Oyster Card is only £1.30 peak time, and caps out at £4. Children aged 15 and under ride free, but a photo bus pass is required for 14- and 15-year-olds. Most Central London buses require that you buy your bus ticket from a ticket machine at a bus stop before boarding; these machines take exact change only. If there is no machine at your bus stop (a rarity in Central London), you can pay the driver or conductor in cash (use small bills or coins only).

Double-decker buses are entered from the front. Pay the driver with cash, show your bus ticket, or your Travelcard, or touch your Oyster Card to the card reader as you board.

Night buses are the only way to get around by public transport after the Tube stops operating. Be sure that there is an "N" bus listed on your bus stop's route or you'll wait in vain until morning.

The newer "bendy buses" are single-deckers with dual carriages.

You may enter these from any open door, but you must touch your Oyster Card to one of the yellow card readers throughout the bus, or you may be fined £20 on the spot. Inspectors often board these buses to catch fare evaders.

By Taxi

All airports and train stations have well-marked areas for London's legendary black cabs, many of which are now colored with advertising, but are still the same distinctive model that holds five people. You can hail a taxi anywhere, on any street, except in certain no-stopping zones marked by red lines along the curb. Available taxis will have a lit sign on top of the cab. Taxis can also be requested by phone, but you will pay more.

Only black cabs, whose drivers have undergone rigorous training known as "the Knowledge," are allowed to cruise the streets for fares. Don't get into cruising mini-cabs, which can legally pick up only those passengers who have booked them by telephone. Black cabs have metered fares (the minimum fare has remained at £2.20, even though the average fare is now well over £10), and surcharges are assessed after 8pm and on weekends. Mini-cab charges should be negotiated in advance.

To book a black cab, call **Radio Taxis** (☎ **020/7272-0272**; www.radiotaxis.co.uk) or **Dial-a-Cab** (☎ **020/7253-5000**; www.dialacab.co.uk). For a minicab, call **Addison Lee** (☎ **0844/800-6677**; www.addisonlee.com).

Fast **Facts**

APARTMENT RENTALS **Central London Apartments** (☎ **0845/644-2714**; www.central-london-apartments.com) offers serviced

apartments in various locations throughout the city. **Home from Home** (☎ **020/7233-8111**; www.homefromhome.co.uk) has a good website that displays all kinds of apartments in numerous London neighborhoods.

ATMS Also known locally as "cashpoints" or "holes in the wall," ATMs are everywhere, and most use global networks such as Cirrus and PLUS. Note that you may be charged a fee by your bank for withdrawing pounds from your foreign currency account.

BABYSITTING Reputable babysitting agencies with vetted employees include **Sitters** (☎ 0800/389-0038; www.sitters.co.uk) and **Universal Aunts** (☎ 020/7738-8937; www.universalaunts.co.uk). Rates are about £7 per hour during the day and £6 per hour in the evening. Hotel guests must pay a £10 booking fee and reasonable transportation costs.

B&BS **The Bed and Breakfast Club** (☎ 0239/263-1313; www.thebedandbreakfastclub.co.uk) and **Uptown Reservations** (☎ 020/7937-2001; www.uptownres.co.uk) are two good reservation companies that offer lovely accommodation in private homes in good neighborhoods.

BANKING HOURS Most banks are open Monday through Friday from 9am to 5pm; some have limited Saturday open hours.

BIKE RENTALS Cycling opportunities increased dramatically in 2010 with the launch of the **Barclays Cycle Hire Scheme**—more popularly known as Boris Bikes after the Mayor. Anyone can hire a bike from one of hundreds of docking stations dotted across town. You can return the bike to any station, making the scheme perfect for short trips. Charges are made up of a fixed access fee—£1 per day or £5 per week—and a usage fee—it's free for 30 minutes, £1 for an hour, £6 for 2 hours, £15 for 3 hours. Buy access with a credit or debit card at the docking station or join online at www.tfl.gov.uk/roadusers/cycling/14808.aspx.

London Bicycle Tour Company, Gabriel's Wharf, South Bank (☎ 020/7928-6838; www.londonbicycle.com) rents a wide variety of bikes. Rates start at £3.50 per hour and £20 per day, and £40 for three days.

BUSINESS HOURS Stores generally open at 9am and close around 6pm Monday through Saturday, though they may stay open until 7 or 8pm one night a week (usually Thurs). Sunday opening hours are typically 11am or noon to 5pm, though some places may open longer. Post offices are open 9am to 5:30pm on weekdays.

CLIMATE See "The Weather," earlier in this chapter.

CONSULATES & EMBASSIES American Embassy, 24 Grosvenor Sq. (☎ 020/7499-9000; www.usembassy.org.uk). **Canadian High Commission,** Canada House, 1 Trafalgar Sq. (☎ 020/7258-6600; www.canadainternational.gc.ca). **Australian High Commission,** Australia House, Strand (☎ 020/7379-4334; www.uk.embassy.gov.au). **Irish Embassy,** 17 Grosvenor Place (☎ 020/7235-2171; www.embassyofireland.co.uk). **New Zealand High Commission,** New Zealand House, 80 Haymarket (☎ 020/7930-8422; www.nzembassy.com/united-kingdom).

CUSTOMS Check **www.hmrc.gov.uk** for what foreign visitors may bring into London. For specifics on what you can bring home with you, check with your own country's customs authority.

DENTISTS **24 Hour Emergency Dental Treatment** Branches at 102 Baker St. and three other locations (☎ 020/8748-9365; www.24houremergencydentist.co.uk). Delivers just what its name promises.

DINING Breakfasts range from the traditional 'full English' of fried eggs, bacon, sausage, beans, grilled tomato, and toast to a more Continental menu of croissants, baguettes, and coffee. If your hotel doesn't include breakfast in its rates, going to a cafe instead will likely be cheaper. Most cafes open from 8am to 8pm. Most restaurants open for lunch from noon to 3pm, and for dinner from 6 to 10 or 11pm. Dress codes have become much more relaxed, and except at very expensive restaurants and hotel dining rooms no one will raise an eyebrow at casual clothing. You will encounter general disapproval if you bring small children to the fanciest restaurants, especially at dinnertime.

Many London restaurants take reservations via the Internet through **www.toptable.com**. You can also ask your hotel's concierge for help when you arrive or when you call to reserve your room.

DOCTORS A number of on-call doctor services can treat you and dispense medicine at your lodgings, or you can go to them. **Doctorcall,** 121 Harley St. (☎ **0844/257-9507;** www.doctorcall.co.uk) and **Pharmacentre,** 149 Edgware Rd. (☎ **0808/ 208-5720;** www.pharmacentre. com) are in Central London and make house calls.

ELECTRICITY Britain uses a 220–240 volt system and alternating current (AC); its electrical plugs have three pins. European appliances will require only a plug adapter, but American 110-volt appliances will need both a transformer and an adapter or they will fry and blow a fuse. Most laptops have built-in electrical transformers, but will need an adapter plug.

EMERGENCIES Call ☎ **999** for accidents and dire medical emergencies free of charge from any phone.

Hospitals with emergency rooms (known as Accident and Emergency departments, or A&E) in Central London include **Charing Cross Hospital,** Fulham Palace Road, Hammersmith (☎ **020/3311-1001**), **Chelsea & Westminster Hospital,** 369 Fulham Road, Chelsea (☎ **020/ 8746-8000**), **St. Mary's Hospital,** Praed Street, Paddington (☎ **020/ 3312-6666**), and **Guy's & St. Thomas's Hospital,** Lambeth Palace Road, Lambeth (☎ **020/ 7188-7188**).

EVENT LISTINGS Good sources of event and entertainment listings include *Time Out,* the *London Evening Standard,* and the Saturday and Sunday supplements in London's daily newspapers.

FAMILY TRAVEL Look for items tagged with a **kids** icon in this book. Most British hotels accommodate families; all but the poshest restaurants are usually family-friendly. The London Tourist Board has a section on its website dedicated to families (www.visitlondon.com/attractions/ family) that provides information on family-friendly attractions, events, and restaurants, and offers discounts on various goods and services. For more detailed information, pick up *Frommer's London with Kids* (Wiley, Inc.) at your local bookstore.

GAY & LESBIAN TRAVELERS London has one of the most active lesbian and gay scenes in the world. The **London Lesbian & Gay Switchboard** (☎ **020/7837-7324;** www. llgs.org.uk) provides advice on everything from gay-friendly lodging to entertainment.

HOLIDAYS Bank holidays, on which most shops and all banks, museums, public buildings, and services are closed, are as follows: New Year's Day, Good Friday (the Fri before Easter), Easter Monday, May Day (first Mon in May), Spring Break (last Mon in May), Summer Break (last Mon in Aug), Christmas Day, and Boxing Day (Dec 26).

INSURANCE Check your existing insurance policies and credit card coverage before buying travel insurance. You may already be covered for lost luggage, canceled tickets, or medical expenses. If you aren't covered, expect to pay 5% to 8% of your trip's cost for insurance.

INTERNET CAFES Though the number of cybercafes has shrunk slightly since the spread of Wi-Fi and smartphones, you'll still find them on most high streets. To find a cafe near you, check **www.london online.co.uk/Cybercafes/**.

The good news for those who've brought their computers or smartphones with them is that Wi-Fi is growing ever more prevalent. Hotel rates can be exorbitant, but free Wi-Fi isn't hard to find. The cafe chains Costa Coffee (www.costa. co.uk), Pret a Manger (www.pret. com), and the ubiquitous Starbucks (http://starbucks.co.uk) offer free Wi-Fi to their customers.

LOST PROPERTY Be sure to tell all your credit card companies the minute you discover your wallet has been lost or stolen, and file a report at the nearest police station (your insurance company may require a police report before covering any claims). If you've lost all forms of photo ID, call your consulate and airline and explain the situation. It's always best to keep copies of your credit card numbers and passport information in a separate location in case you lose the real items.

For help in finding property lost on London public transport (buses, Tube, and taxis), call the **TFL Lost Property Office,** 200 Baker St. (☎ **0845/330-9882**); if you've lost something on an overland train, call the main terminal that serves the train on which you lost your

property, or call the above number for help.

MAIL & POSTAGE Stamps for a small letter mailed inside the U.K. cost 46p for first class and 36p for second class. Postage for postcards and letters sent outside the U.K. to Europe is 68p and 76p to the rest of the world. You can pay for and print out postage at **www.royalmail. com**. Most newsagents carry stamps, and the city's distinctive red mailboxes are plentiful. The central post office in Trafalgar Square is open from 8:30am to 6:30pm Monday to Friday, and 9am to 5:30pm Saturday.

MONEY England clings stubbornly to its pound sterling and pence. £1 consists of 100 pence (pennies). There are one- and two-pound coins; silvery 50p, 20p, 10p, and 5p coins; and copper 2p and 1p coins. Banknotes are issued in denominations of £50 (red), £20 (lavender), £10 (orange), and £5 (blue).

Foreign money can be exchanged at most banks and bureaux de change, but you'll be assessed a hefty surcharge or get terrible conversion rates. If you want to arrive with a few pounds in hand, get them from your bank before you leave home. ATMs (known locally as cashpoints) are located all over the city and offer the best exchange rates; find out your daily withdrawal limit before you leave home. At the time of writing, £1 was worth $1.64. For the most up-to-date currency conversion information, go to **www.xe.com**.

Many stores in London will not take traveler's checks, and those that do often charge stiff fees. It's best to stick to cash and credit cards, though most banks assess a 2% fee above the 1% fee charged by Visa, MasterCard, or American Express for currency conversions.

Be sure to notify your credit card companies before leaving for London so they don't become suspicious when the card is used numerous times in London and block your account.

PARKING Parking in London is difficult, even for those who have paid for a resident parking permit (yet another reason not to drive here). Metered spaces have time limits of 1 to 4 hours and are hard to find.

Garages (parking lots) are expensive, but plentiful. Look for signs that say **NCP** (for National Car Park); call ☎ **0845/050-7080** or check out **www.ncp.co.uk** for locations and more information.

Always check any warning signs on streets for info on temporary parking suspensions. Parking violations are punished with a hefty fine, tire clamping, or the removal of your car to an impound lot. If your car has been towed, call ☎ **020/7747-4747.**

PASSES The **London Pass** (www.londonpass.com) offers discounted travel on public transport and free admission to 55 of London's high-priced attractions, as well as other useful discounts. Pass package prices are as follows: 1 day £52 adults, £32 children; 3 days £96 adults, £58 children; 6 days £145 adults, £93 children. You don't need the London pass for most museums as they are free, but you will save money if you can cram a few fee-charging attractions into 1 or 3 days.

PASSPORTS Citizens of the United States, Canada, Ireland, Australia, and New Zealand need only a valid passport to enter England.

Always make a copy of your passport's information page and keep it separate from your passport in case of loss or theft. For emergency passport replacement, contact your country's embassy or consulate (see "Consulates & Embassies," on p 163).

PHARMACIES These "chemists" can fill a valid doctor's prescription. **Bliss Chemist,** 5–6 Marble Arch (☎ **020/7723-6116**) stays open till midnight, while **Zafash Pharmacy,** 233–235 Old Brompton Rd., Earls Court (☎ **020/7373-2798**), is open 24 hours. The leading drugstore chain in the U.K., **Boots** (www.boots.com), has branches all over London.

SAFETY London has its share of violent crime, just as any other major city does—its biggest crime-related problems are public intoxication and muggings—but it is usually quite safe for visitors as long as you take common-sense precautions. Good safety tips include:

- Use your hotel safe.
- Be alert when withdrawing money from ATMs; don't take out more cash than you need, and don't carry large sums around.
- Guard your valuables in public places and keep your wallet in an inner pocket. Pickpockets operate in all the major tourist zones.
- Don't leave pocketbooks dangling from chairs in restaurants or Internet cafes; use a purse that closes securely.
- Avoid conspicuous displays of expensive jewelry.
- Avoid the upper decks of buses late at night. Take a cab if you can afford it.
- Stay alert in high-end shopping areas: Bags from luxury shops are a tip-off to thieves.
- There's safety in numbers—don't wander alone in Soho or the West End very late at night. And stay out of parks after dark.
- Don't hop in a minicab hailed off the street. Stick to official black cabs (p 162).

SENIOR TRAVELERS   Discounts (concessions) for seniors over 64 are available (with proof of age) for museums and some entertainment.

SMOKING   Smoking is prohibited in shops, all public transportation, and all public buildings. It's also forbidden inside restaurants, pubs, and bars (although these may have dedicated outside smoking areas). Tobacco is expensive in the U.K., so if you smoke, bring your cigarettes from home or buy them in the airport duty-free shop.

SPECTATOR SPORTS   London is crazy for football (that's soccer to you Americans out there) and is home to several professional teams. One of the best places to watch the English lose their decorum (although tickets are hard to come by) is at **Chelsea Football Club,** Stamford Bridge, Fulham Road (☎ **0871/984-1955;** www.chelseafc.com). Wear blue and you'll fit right in. For a more genteel (albeit confusing) experience, try watching a cricket match at the sport's most hallowed field—**Lords Cricket Club,** St. John's Wood Road (☎ **020/7616-8500;** www.lords.org).

The most sacred annual London sporting event is June's **Lawn Tennis Championships at Wimbledon** (☎ **020/8971-2473** for tickets; 020/8944-1066 for information; www.wimbledon.com). Check the website for details on how to enter your name for the January lottery tickets. Same-day seats to the outside courts are available, but you'll wait in very long line-ups.

TAXES   A 20% value-added tax (VAT) is added on hotel bills and restaurant checks, merchandise, and most services. Non-E.U. visitors are eligible for partial VAT refunds (for more information, see p 86). Note that price tags on items in stores already include the VAT (except in some antique shops). Gasoline (petrol) in Britain is taxed at 25%.

TAXIS   See "By Taxi," on p 162.

TELEPHONES   London has three types of public pay phones: Those accepting only coins, those accepting only phone cards (Cardphones), and those that take both phone cards and most major credit cards. Phone cards can be purchased in several denominations (£2–£20) at most newsstands and post offices. The minimum charge for a local call is 40p.

London's city code is **020,** but you don't need to dial it within city limits; just dial the eight-digit number. To call London from the rest of the U.K., you must dial the 020 followed by the number. When calling London from abroad, dial the international code (011 from North America, 0011 from Australia, and 00 from New Zealand), followed by 44 (England's country code), followed by 20, and then the eight-digit number.

When calling abroad from London, dial 00, the country code, the area code, and then the number. Directory assistance in London can be reached by calling ☎ **118 180,** but try to dial numbers direct, because connection costs through directory assistance companies are high.

TICKETS   Most West End theatres keep a few seats in reserve to sell on the day of a performance. If you're set on seeing a specific show or event (especially the ballet or opera), book your tickets in advance (for a small service fee) through **Londontown** (www.londontown.com), **Ticketmaster** (www.ticketmaster.co.uk), or **Keith Prowse** (www.keithprowse.com). You can also try calling the box office directly.

You can get half-price theatre tickets at the free-standing **tkts** kiosk on the south side of Leicester Square for same-day performances of selected shows. For more information on buying tickets in advance, see p 137.

TIPPING   Tipping is much less common in the U.K. than in many other countries (notably the U.S.A.). It is not usual to tip chambermaids (though you may certainly do so), bartenders in pubs, or taxi drivers—unless they've helped you with your luggage, in which case a 10% tip should suffice. Hairdressers should be tipped 10%. Hotel porters should get £1 per bag; doormen should get £1 for hailing you a cab. Check restaurant checks for an automatic service charge, which usually runs around 12% to 15%. If service hasn't been included, tip your waiter 12 to 15%, as long as you feel the service merited it. You aren't expected to tip at a pub unless table service is provided.

TOILETS   Clean public toilets can be found in most shopping centers and major railway and Tube stations. Some are free, though some charge around 30p for use. Pubs and hotels don't get too fussy if you discreetly nip in to use the loo (especially if you buy a drink first). Department stores have public restrooms, usually stashed on high floors to discourage traffic. For more information on public restrooms (loos), see p 64.

TOURIST OFFICES   Drop into the official **London Tourist Board Visitor Centre**, 1 Lower Regent St. (☎ **0870/156-6366;** www.visit london.com; Tube: Piccadilly Circus), for information in eight languages, useful pamphlets, maps, Travelcards, and souvenirs. The center also has a decent cafe and offers currency exchange and Internet access. It's open from 9:30am to 6:30pm weekdays (till 6pm Oct–Mar), and 10am to 4pm weekends.

TOURIST TRAPS & SCAMS   The half-price theatre-ticket shops around Soho are rip-offs (they tag on a heavy commission for poor seats), and most tickets sold on the street are counterfeit; use only the official half-price ticket booth (tkts, p 137) at the south end of Leicester Square. Don't buy from the street peddlers selling perfume and accessories. See "Safety," above.

TOURS   Two similar companies offer good orientation tours of the city from the vantage of a double-decker bus: **London Big Bus** (☎ **020/ 7233-9533;** www.bigbustours.com) and **Original London Sightseeing Tour** (☎ **020/8877-1722;** www.the originaltour.com). Tickets, good for 24 hours, allow visitors to hop on and off buses that stop at most of Central London's major attractions (buses run every 15–30 min.). Both companies' tours cost in the region of £27 and take about 2 hours; audio commentary is available in a number of languages. The Big Bus tour ticket also covers a small selection of themed walking tours.

Black Taxi Tours of London (☎ **020/7935-9363;** www.blacktaxi tours.co.uk) offers personalized 2-hour tours in a genuine black cab for up to five people for £115. The cabs can venture where buses cannot, making it easier to get off the tourist trail.

For walking tours of London that are geared to particular interests or themes, you can't do better than **The Original London Walks** (☎ **020/7624-3978;** www.walks. com). Expert guides lead visitors on tours ranging from ghost walks to strolls through literary London to historic pub crawls. Walks cost £8 each.

If you want to tour London via the Thames, **City Cruises** (☎ 020/7740-0400; www.citycruises.com) runs sightseeing trips in modern riverboats equipped with audio commentary in six languages. Tours depart from Westminster, Waterloo, and Tower piers; they range in duration from 30 minutes to 2½ hours.

Many of the city's museums and royal palaces offer daily gallery talks and themed tours inspired by the various objects in their collections.

TRAVELERS WITH DISABILITIES
Most of London's major museums are fitted with wheelchair ramps.

Discounts for travelers with disabilities, known as "concessions," are offered by many attractions and theatres. **Tourism for All** (☎ 0845/124-9971; www.tourismforall.org.uk) offers loads of information and advice for travelers with disabilities visiting Britain. Visitors with disabilities planning to travel via public transportation should order *Access in London,* an essential guide for travelers with disabilities, put out by **Artsline**; it can be ordered at **www.accessinlondon.org**.

VAT   See "Taxes," above.

A Brief **History**

A.D. **43**   Romans invade England and settle Londinium.

61   Queen Boadicea sacks Londinium in a brutal but unsuccessful rebellion against Rome.

200   Romans fortify the city with a wall.

410   Roman troops abandon London as the Empire falls.

600   King Ethelbert builds first St. Paul's Church on ruins of Temple of Diana.

800   Vikings raid Britain.

885   Alfred the Great captures London from the Vikings.

1042   Edward the Confessor is crowned king of England and begins work on Westminster Abbey.

1066   William the Conqueror is crowned king of England in Westminster Abbey after the Battle of Hastings. London becomes seat of political power.

1078   Construction of the Tower of London begins.

1176–1209   London Bridge is built, the first permanent stone crossing linking the two banks of the Thames.

1192   Henry FitzAilwin is elected first lord mayor of London.

1215   Magna Carta is signed by King John.

1240   First Parliament is convened at Westminster.

1348   First outbreak of the Black Death plagues London.

1381   Wat Tyler's Peasant Revolt is mercilessly crushed.

1476   William Caxton, the first English printer, revolutionizes English printing and makes Fleet Street the country's publishing center.

1599   Shakespeare's first play is performed at the Globe Theatre.

1605   The Gunpowder Plot to destroy Parliament is thwarted on November 5.

1642   The Puritan government orders the closure of playhouses such as the Rose and the Globe.

1649   Charles I is beheaded at Whitehall.

1653   Oliver Cromwell is made Lord Protector of the Realm. Puritan rule closes London's theatres, brothels, and gaming halls.

1665   Outbreak of bubonic plague kills 100,000 Londoners.

1666   Great Fire of London sweeps through the city.

1667   Christopher Wren begins work on St. Paul's Cathedral; attempts to redraw London's map are abandoned.

1675   The Royal Observatory is founded in Greenwich.

1688   James II is banished during the Glorious Revolution; William and Mary move into Kensington Palace.

1694   First Bank of England is established in the City of London.

1735   Dr. Samuel Johnson moves to London and becomes a fixture on the coffeehouse circuit.

1759   The British Museum is opened to the public.

1810   London's first Indian restaurant opens.

1829   Robert Peel sets up Metropolitan Police force, known as "bobbies" in his honor.

1836   Charles Dickens publishes *The Pickwick Papers* and becomes London's favorite novelist.

1837   Eighteen-year-old Queen Victoria ascends the throne and moves into Buckingham Palace.

1851   Great Exhibition takes place in Hyde Park, financing the development of South Kensington.

1854   Cholera epidemic in London results in improved sewage system.

1857   Victoria & Albert (V&A) Museum opens.

1860   London's first public flushing toilet opens.

1863   London opens the world's first Underground Transit System (Tube).

1908   For the first time, London hosts the Olympic games at White City.

1909   American Gordon Selfridge opens London's iconic department store.

1914   World War I starts; zeppelins drop bombs on London.

1939–45   World War II air raids kill thousands in London and destroy much of the city's infrastructure.

1948   London hosts the first postwar Olympic Games.

1951   Festival of Britain held on the South Bank.

1953   Queen Elizabeth II is crowned in Westminster Abbey.

1956   The Routemaster red double-decker bus takes to the streets.

1963   Youth-quake in London: The Beatles and the Rolling Stones rule the day.

1981   Prince Charles marries Lady Diana Spencer in St. Paul's Cathedral.

1986   The M25, London's orbital highway, opens.

1994   London is linked to Paris by rail via the Channel Tunnel.

1997   London mourns the death of Princess Diana.

2000   Traditional pigeon feeding in Trafalgar Square is outlawed.

2002   London celebrates Queen Elizabeth II's Golden Jubilee.

2005   London wins bid for the 2012 Olympics; 55 die in July 7 terrorist attacks on London transport.

2008   "Red" Ken Livingstone is ousted as Mayor of London by Boris Johnson. Boris introduces bike-hire scheme to London's streets.

2011   Prince William marries Kate Middleton in Westminster Abbey.

2012   London hosts the Olympic Games for the third time (the first time with the Paralympic games).

London's **Architecture**

Norman Period: 1066–1200
The oldest-surviving style of architecture in London dates back to the time of William the Conqueror, when the Normans overran England. Thick walls and masonry were used to support the large interiors needed to accommodate the churchgoing masses. The heavy construction usually gave Norman buildings a dark and foreboding air.

Characteristics of the period include:

• Thick walls with small windows

• Round weight-bearing arches

• Huge piers (square stacks of masonry)

• Chevrons—zigzagging decorations surrounding doorways or wrapped around columns

The Tower of London's **White Tower,** built by William the Conqueror, is a textbook example of a Norman-style castle. **St. John's Chapel** within the White Tower is one of the few remaining Norman-style churches in England.

Gothic: 1200–1550
French in origin, the fairy-tale Gothic style introduced innovations that allowed builders to transfer weight away from a structure's walls so they could be taller and thinner.

The style also allowed for the use of larger windows, which allowed more natural light to reach a building's interior.

In addition to the pointed arch, Gothic construction features:

• Vaulted ceilings, using cross vaulting (an "X" design) and fan vaulting (a more conic design)

• Flying buttresses, free-standing exterior pillars that helped support the building's weight

• Carved tracery stonework connecting windows

• Stained-glass windows

You need look no further than **Westminster Abbey,** built in the mid-14th century, for a perfect London example of the Gothic style.

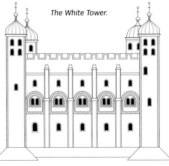
The White Tower.

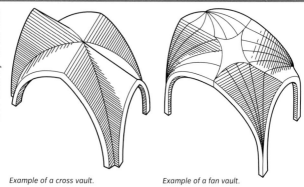

Example of a cross vault.

Example of a fan vault.

Renaissance: 1550–1650

The Renaissance style, involving proportion and mathematical precision enlivened by decoration, was imported from the Continent by the great Inigo Jones, who was greatly influenced by Italian Palladianism.

Characteristics of Renaissance architecture include:

- A sense of proportion
- A reliance on symmetry
- The use of classical columns—Doric, Ionic, and Corinthian

Top examples of this style include the **Banqueting Hall at Whitehall** and the **arcade** of Covent Garden, both designed by Inigo Jones.

Baroque: 1650–1750

Baroque architects Christopher Wren and Nicholas Hawksmoor had unrivalled opportunities to practice their craft in London when the Great Fire of 1666 provided a clean palette on which to replace medieval wooden structures.

The prime features of the more fanciful baroque style include:

- Classical forms marked by grand curving lines
- Decoration with playful carvings

St. Paul's Cathedral, with its massive dome and complex exterior decor, is Wren's crowning achievement and the finest example of English baroque architecture in London.

The Classical Orders.

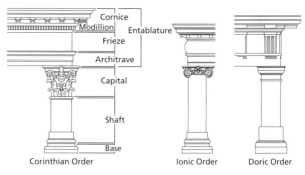

Neoclassical & Greek Revival: 1750–1837

Neoclassicism was an 18th-century reaction to the busy nature of baroque architecture. Notable characteristics of neoclassical architecture include:

- Clean, elegant lines, with balance and symmetry
- Use of classical Greek columns
- Crescent layouts (half-circles of identical stone houses with tall windows)

Sir John Soane's Museum and John Nash's curving white stucco **Cumberland Terrace** in Regent's Park are exemplars of these styles.

Gothic Revival: 1750–1900

As industrialization began its inexorable march on London, artists and architects looked back to a simpler and more romantic fairy-tale period for their inspiration.

The features that marked the Gothic Revival style include:

- A confusion of spires, arches, and decorative detail
- Buildings constructed on a grand scale

The **Palace of Westminster,** home to the British Parliament, is the farthest-reaching exponent of this style; the most compact is the **Albert Memorial** in Hyde Park.

St. Paul's Cathedral.

20th & Early 21st Century: 1900–Present

The 20th century saw London expanding into its suburbs with uninspired architecture. The Blitz was the period's (far more tragic) version of the Great Fire, and rebuilding took place with postwar austerity. The ugly, utilitarian style of South Bank's **Royal Festival Hall** is known as **Brutalism. Post-modernism** is a softening of that style, applying the whimsy of the past to the modern, which brought about the inside-out **Lloyd's Building** and the **Gherkin Building.** The best marriage of old and new can be seen in the covered **Great Court** of the British Museum, which managed to put a new hat on an old friend without making it look silly.

The Palace of Westminster.

The Wren Style

One of the great geniuses of his age (and London's greatest architect), Sir Christopher Wren (1632–1723) was a professor of astronomy at Oxford before becoming an architect. After the Great Fire of London in 1666, Wren was chosen to rebuild the devastated city and its many churches, including St. Paul's, on which work began in 1675. His designs had great originality, and he became known for his spatial effects and his impressive fusion of classical and baroque. He believed in classical stability and repose, yet he liked to enliven his churches with baroque whimsy and fantasy. Nothing better represents the Wren style than the facade of St. Paul's (p 13, ⑩), for which he combined classical columns, reminiscent of Greek temples, with baroque decorations and adornments.

Useful London Terms & Language

London has one of the world's most famous argots. **Cockney rhyming slang** emerged from the East End during the 19th century, and consists of words and phrases constructed using a rhyme—a creative process that makes what you're talking about both less likely to be understood by the uninitiated, and more likely to be humorous. To make the dialect still more obscure, the word that was the original object of the rhyme is often omitted. For example, "bread" meaning money derives from a rhyme with "bread and honey" and "ruby" meaning curry derives from "Ruby Murray," a 1950s singer. Although some words and phrases have entered common parlance— "barnet," from "Barnet Fair," meaning

hair is another—you're unlikely to hear too much pure rhyming slang as you travel the city.

However, London does have a vocabulary of its own—some of it derived from or influenced by Cockney, some disparagingly referred to as "mockney," some related to products, places, and produce that are peculiar to the city, and some just plain slang. You may also notice the liberal use of the F-word on London's streets. Although it certainly isn't considered a polite word, its impact on the local listener is more diluted than in most other English-speaking cities.

Below is a glossary of some London words and phrases you may encounter.

bangers sausages; usually paired with mashed potato for "bangers and mash"
banging good; usually applied to music
barking crazy or mad; coined from a former asylum in the eastern suburb of Barking

barney   an argument or disagreement

bedlam   madness; as in "the roads are bedlam today"; a corruption of "Bethle-hem," an asylum formerly at the corner of Moorgate and London Wall, in the City

black cab   an official London black taxi, as opposed to a private hire "minicab"; only black cabs are permitted to tout for fares kerbside

Boris bikes   rental cycles that are part of the Barclays Cycle Hire scheme (see p 163); named after Mayor Boris Johnson, who presided over the scheme's introduction in 2010

butcher's   a look (from Cockney "butcher's hook"); as in "can I have a butcher's?"

BYO   short for "bring your own"; a restaurant that doesn't sell alcoholic drinks but will happily open any you bring along, sometimes for a small corkage fee

circus   a (usually circular) coming together of streets, as at Piccadilly Circus and Finsbury Circus

clink   a prison; after the former Clink Prison, on the South Bank

damage   the cost or bill; as in "what's the damage?"

dodgy   not to be trusted, suspect; as in "that £20 note looks dodgy"

dosh   money; also "bread" or "dough"

gaff   home; "back to my gaff" means "back to my place"

G 'n' T   gin and tonic; often served with "ice and a slice," i.e. an ice cube and a lemon wedge

gastrocaff   a fashionable cafe that nevertheless serves traditional English fried breakfasts

geezer   a man; also "bloke" or "fella"

greasy spoon   the opposite of "gastrocaff": a basic cafe known for fried food

gutted   extremely disappointed; as in "I'm gutted that Arsenal beat Spurs last night"

IPA   India Pale Ale; a type of hoppy, light-colored English ale first brewed in the 18th century

lager   straw-colored, fizzy light beer such as Budweiser and Foster's, served colder than traditional ales (although it's a myth that English beers are served "warm"; they should appear at cool cellar temperature)

liquor   green parsley sauce served in traditional pie and mash shops

naff   cheap looking, or unfashionable

Porter   type of dark, strong ale once popular with London dockers; London brewers Fuller's and Meantime both brew contemporary versions

pint   both a measure of beer and a general term for having a drink; as in "do you fancy going for a pint later?"

quid   one pound; "10 quid" or "a tenner" is £10

subway   a pedestrian underpass; the underground railway is known as "the Tube"

wally   a type of pickled gherkin, often paired with fish and chips

Photo **Credits**

Front cover (L–R): © Eric Nathan / Alamy Images; © Alistair Laming / Alamy Images; © Eric Nathan / Alamy Images.

Back cover: © Ellie Kurttz.

Interior images:

© Anne Ackermann / Aurora: p viii, p 4 bottom, p 7, p 11, p 12, p 16, p 17, p 21, p 22, p 24, p 37, p 51, p 59, p 65 top, p 68, p 74, p 85, p 87, p 95, p 108.

© Anthony Woods: p 4 top, p 6 bottom, p 13, p 25, p 31, p 35, p 39, p 40, p 44, p 55, p 56, p 57, p 60 top, p 61, p 65 bottom, p 72, p 78, p 82, p 83 top, p 89–p 94, p 112, p 127, p 129, p 135.

© The Berkeley: p 120.

© The Connaught: p 111, p 122, p 149.

© Elisabeth Blanchet: p 5, p 6 top, p 10, p 18, p 19, p 27, p 29, p 32, p 41, p 45, p 47, p 49, p 54, p 60 bottom, p 64, p 67, p 73, p 80, p 83 bottom, p 86, p 110, p 130, p 155.

© Firmdale Hotels: p 139, p 150.

© Gordon Ramsay Holdings: p 103.

© The Goring, Belgravia, London: p 152.

© Jill Emeny / Frommer's: p 124.

© jmanz / Frommers.com Community: p 125.

© Jonathan Gregson: p 107.

© keiko oikawa: p 109.

© The Langham, London: p 119.

© Paul Close: p 136.

© Phil Ashley: p 96.

© Porters: p 104.

© Searcys: p 105.

Courtesy of Claridge's: p 148.

Courtesy of Ronnie Scott's: p 123.

Courtesy of The Thistle Piccadilly: p 140, p 153.